Contents

KU-192-738

COLLINS GEM GUIDES

BUTTERFLIES AND MOTHS

Brian Hargreaves

Michael Chinery

COLLINS
London and Glasgow

First published 1981

© Michael Chinery and Brian Hargreaves 1981

ISBN 0 00 458808 8

Colour reproduction by Adroit Photo-Litho Ltd, Birmingham

Filmset by Jolly & Barber Ltd, Rugby

Printed and bound by Wm Collins Sons and Co Ltd, Glasgow

Reprint 10 9 8 7 6 5 4 3

How to Use this Book

The butterflies and moths illustrated in this book are just a small selection of the species living in Europe, but they include most of the really common and widely distributed ones found in Western Europe. There are also a few less common, but very striking and conspicuous species, and so, with the aid of this book, you should be able to identify most of the species that you see around you. English and scientific names are given where possible, but non-British species often have no English name. Butterflies in the centre of each spread show upper side on left and underside on the right.

Size. Unless otherwise stated, all insects are shown at their natural size, but some of the butterflies in the centre of the spreads are slightly reduced. Butterflies of 2nd and 3rd broods are often much smaller than 1st-brood insects.

Sexes are alike unless otherwise stated. Most illustrations are of males ($\male$). Females are denoted by $\female$.

Range is given in a very simplified form. Northern Europe (N) is taken to be the area north of 58°N: Central Europe (C) includes Britain (B) and all areas down to 45°N: Southern Europe (S) is south of 45°N. Insects do not occur everywhere within the range – only where habitat is suitable. Unless otherwise stated, all species occur in Britain.

Flight times cover the whole range of the insect and may be much more restricted in northern areas, where the insects generally appear much later.

Introduction

The butterflies and moths are among the most colourful and popular members of the insect world. They belong to one of the largest groups, with about 165,000 known species. About 5,000 occur in Europe. The group is technically known as the Lepidoptera, a name which means 'scale wings' and refers to the minute scales which clothe the wings and give them their colourful patterns. The scales are only loosely attached and readily come off when the insects are handled.

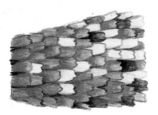

A much-enlarged drawing of the overlapping scales which clothe a butterfly's wing.

One of the commonest questions asked about this group of insects is 'What is the difference between butterflies and moths?'. It sounds a simple question, but the answer is not a simple one, for there is no single difference between all the butterflies on the

The small pearl-bordered fritillary – a typical butterfly showing the clubbed antennae and bright colours.

one hand and all the moths on the other. Butterflies are almost entirely day-flying insects, while most moths are nocturnal, but there are plenty of day-flying moths and several of them are brightly coloured and easily mistaken for butterflies. It is often said that the resting attitude will separate the butterflies from the moths: butterflies normally rest with their wings closed vertically above the back, while moths generally hold their wings out to the sides or roof-wise over the body. But there are exceptions: some skipper butterflies, for example, hold their wings roof-wise over the body, while certain geometrid moths, such as some thorns, perch with their wings

The grey dagger moth with its wings in the roof-wise resting position characteristic of many moths.

held vertically over the body. The antennae are the best guide: all butterflies have small knobs on the ends of their antennae, whereas moth antennae are usually thread-like or feathery. But even this rule has its exceptions, for the day-flying burnet moths have distinctly clubbed antennae and are regularly mistaken for butterflies. It is necessary to look at the wings to establish that these insects really are moths. Look at the underside and you will find a slender bristle sprouting from the 'shoulder' of the hind wing and running forward to engage in a little clip on the front wing. This bristle is called a frenulum and its job is to join the two wings and to ensure that they beat in unison. Many other moths have a frenulum,

The frenulum of a burnet moth, showing how it links front and hind wings together.

but none of the European butterflies has one: in fact, only one butterfly in the world – an Australian skipper – is known to have a frenulum. Butterflies link their wings together simply by having a large overlap.

Having said all this, it must be pointed out that the distinction between butterflies and moths is quite artificial and unimportant. Most European languages make no basic distinction between them: in French, for example, butterflies are *papillons diurnes* and moths are *papillons nocturnes*. The butterflies number less than 20,000 species and account for only 15 of the 80 or so families of Lepidoptera. All the rest are moths and they differ amongst themselves just as much as they differ from butterflies. The division of the order into butterflies and moths is therefore a very unequal one as well as an artificial one.

Although the butterflies and moths exhibit a very wide variation in size – from about 3mm to 30cm in wingspan – they are remarkably uniform in their structure and habits. Apart from a few female moths which are wingless, the adults all have four scale-covered wings. The other major feature that dis-

A large blue butterfly plunging its proboscis into a flower. The wings are in the typical resting position for a butterfly, although not fully closed.

tinguishes the Lepidoptera from other insects is the long tongue or proboscis. This is a tubular structure and it is actually composed of two horny strips which are deeply grooved on the inner surface. The two halves are linked together by numerous minute hooks and the two grooves come together to form the feeding tube. When not in use, the tongue is coiled up underneath the head, but it is extended by a combination of muscular action and blood pressure as soon as the insect detects food. Nectar from flowers is the main food of both butterflies and moths, although some species also enjoy fruit juices. Some even gather to imbibe fluids from dung, decaying meat, and muddy puddles. The fluids are sucked up through the proboscis in the same way that we suck liquids through a straw, and when the meal is over the proboscis coils up again through its own natural elasticity. A number of moths do not feed in the adult state and have no fully-developed proboscis, but on the other hand there are hawkmoths with tongues up to 10cm long which can reach the nectar deep in the tubular flowers of *Nicotiana* and honeysuckle. A few small moths are pollen-feeders and have chewing mouth-parts instead of sucking tubes.

Males and females look alike in many species and it is not always easy to distinguish the sexes on the external features alone. There are, however, many other species in which males and females are quite different. This is especially true among the butterflies, notable examples being the brimstone and the orange-tip and, of course, the blues – in which the females are brown! Moths tend to be more alike in the two sexes, although there are exceptions: the emperor moth and the gypsy moth, for example, are quite differently coloured in the two sexes, and we have already mentioned that some species have wingless females. Where the sexes are similar, the female can often be recognised by her bulkier body and more rounded hind end. The antennae are also a good guide to the sex of a moth in many species, for they are often very much more feathery in the males. This gives a greater surface area and indicates the importance of scent in finding a mate. Female moths give out a scent, and this is picked up by the males' antennae. The males then fly upwind and eventually find the females. Emperor moths are able to detect the female scent from as much as a kilometre away. Some tropical moths can home in on the females from even greater distances. But not all moths rely on the female's scent to bring them together. The males produce scents in some species, and sight is also used. The male ghost swift's wings are pure white on the upper surface and dull brown below, and as it flies slowly over the vegetation the rhythmic flashing of white attracts the female.

There is no real courtship among moths, but many butterflies perform some kind of courtship display. The two sexes are initially attracted to each other by sight, with unmated individuals – usually the males – flying up to greet anything of about the right size and colour. Scent then takes over, and it is normally the male who produces the most scent among the butterflies. The scent is emitted by special scales called androconia, which may be scattered all over the wings or aggregated into distinct patches known as scent brands or sex brands. These patches readily distinguish the males in many species. Only an unmated female of the same species will respond to the scent and allow courtship to proceed, and the male may finally stimulate her to mate by rubbing his scent-laden wings over her antennae.

The females lay eggs after mating, normally using sense organs on the head and the feet to ensure that

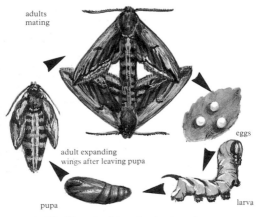

adults mating

eggs

adult expanding wings after leaving pupa

pupa

larva

The life cycle of the privet hawk moth

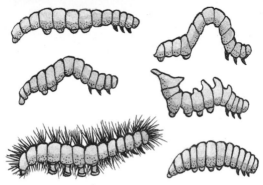

A range of caterpillars showing some of the many variations in shape and in the number of prolegs.

they lay on the right food plant for the ensuing caterpillars, although some moths merely scatter their eggs over the vegetation. The eggs usually hatch in a couple of weeks, but a few species pass the winter in the egg stage. The caterpillars, or larvae, which hatch from the eggs may be hairy or smooth-skinned. All have three pairs of true legs at the front and most have five pairs of stumpy prolegs towards the back. The prolegs on the last segment are called claspers. Some groups of caterpillars have fewer prolegs. The best-known of these are the looper or geometer larvae, which have only two pairs including the claspers. There are no antennae and no compound eyes, and the larvae have biting jaws instead of probosci. With the exception of the few clothes moth larvae, which

13

eat animal fibres, the caterpillars are all herbivorous. Most are leaf-eaters, but there are also caterpillars that eat roots and fruits and some that even chew their way through woody stems.

The young caterpillar feeds voraciously and very soon outgrows its tough skin, which does not grow with the rest of the body. The caterpillar then becomes quiescent for a while and then bursts out of the skin, having grown a new and looser one beneath it. When the new skin has hardened, the caterpillar starts to feed again, and a second moult is soon necessary. A caterpillar may undergo up to eight such moults during its life, but four is the normal number for most species. The larval stage may be over in as little as four weeks, although caterpillars which hatch in late summer often hibernate and complete their growth in spring. Many caterpillars are beautifully camouflaged, often bearing striking resemblances to twigs and thereby escaping the attentions of birds and other enemies. Some are protected by dense coats of irritating hairs, while others have unpleasant tastes and advertise the fact with bold colour patterns – a phenomenon known as warning coloration.

When fully grown, the caterpillar prepares to turn into the chrysalis, or pupa. This is the non-feeding stage during which the larval body is broken down and converted to the adult form. Many moth larvae burrow into the ground and pupate in silk-lined chambers, while others spin silken cocoons among the vegetation or the debris on the ground. As a general rule of thumb, it may be said that hairy

A large tortoiseshell caterpillar clings to a support and gradually rolls back its skin to reveal the chrysalis.

larvae spin cocoons and hairless ones burrow, but there are exceptions to this rule. The pupae themselves are usually bullet-shaped, brown, and shiny. Some butterfly larvae, notably those of the skippers, spin flimsy cocoons at soil level, but the majority of butterfly pupae are naked. Some hang upside-down from the food plant or other support, while others

A variety of butterfly pupae, or chrysalids.

are attached in an upright position and supported by a silken girdle. All are attached to a small pad of silk at the tail end. Being freely exposed in this way, the butterfly pupae need some kind of camouflage and they are often ornately shaped and coloured to blend in with the plants to which they are attached.

When the adult insect, or imago, is ready to emerge, it bursts through the pupal skin and drags itself out. The wings are very small and crumpled at first, but the insect finds a suitable point from which to hang and it begins to pump blood into the wing veins. The wings soon expand and harden, and the mature insect can then fly away. Adult life is generally quite short – perhaps a month or two – but there are some exceptions, as described below.

Butterflies and moths are usually very seasonal in their appearance, but they exhibit a wide range of life cycles. The simplest, known as the single-brooded or univoltine life cycle, is that in which there is just one generation or brood each year: the insects fly for a few weeks at the appropriate season and then disappear until the following year. A typical example is the orange-tip butterfly, which flies and lays its eggs in spring and disappears in June. The larvae pupate by mid-summer and the pupal stage lasts right round until the spring. But not all univoltine species overwinter as pupae: the purple hairstreak butterfly spends the winter in the egg stage, and a great many species hibernate as larvae. A few species hibernate as adults, and the adult stage is then prolonged for as much as nine months. The peacock butterfly is a typical example. It can be seen at garden flowers in late summer and again in the spring. In common with most other butterflies that hibernate as adults, it has very sombre undersides that camouflage it well when it is sleeping in hollow trees, caves, and similar places.

Many butterflies and moths have a bivoltine cycle, with two generations each year. The poplar hawk-moth, for example, emerges from its pupa in May and the females lay eggs. A new generation of moths flies in late summer and their offspring pass the winter as pupae. So the pupal stage lasts for about a month in the summer brood and about eight months in the overwintering brood. Many bivoltine species hibernate as larvae, and some hibernate as adults, thus having three flight periods in a year. The small tortoiseshell butterfly is a good example. Emerging from their pupae in late summer, the adults fly in the autumn and again in early spring. They lay their eggs, and a new generation flies in mid-summer. These are the parents of the new over-wintering generation. The two larval generations are found April/May and July/August.

Very often, a species with just one generation in the northern parts of its range will have two broods further south. Some species have three or even four generations in a year, but individuals of these late broods are often much smaller than those flying earlier in the year.

1. Scarce Swallowtail
Iphiclides podalirius

This handsome and unmistakable insect has a ground colour ranging from white to pale yellow, with female slightly larger. It has a rapid, gliding flight just above head height, and is found March/September in flowery fields and orchards. There are usually two broods. The larva **(1a)** feeds April/October on blackthorn and on various cultivated fruit trees. S. & C. Europe: not B.

2. Southern Swallowtail *Papilio alexanor*
Darker yellows and shorter tails distinguish this species from **1**, and the prominent stripes separate it from the common swallowtail (*P. machaon*). Female is often larger. It flies strongly in flowery meadows April/July and is very fond of thistles. Larva similar to that of *machaon*, feeding on various umbellifers May/September. Mountainous regions of southern Europe, up to 1500m.

1. Swallowtail *Papilio machaon*

This beautiful. insect frequents flowery places April/September. It has a strong, elusive flight, but readily settles on various flowers to drink **(1a)**. There are two or three broods in southern Europe, with summer specimens much paler than spring ones. The larva **(1b)** feeds on wild carrot, fennel, and other umbellifers May/September. If disturbed, it protrudes the osmeterium (arrowed) and emits a strong scent. Most Europe, but very rare in B. (Norfolk Broads only).

2. Corsican Swallowtail *Papilio hospiton*
Very similar to **(1)**, this species can be distinguished by the shorter tails and by the wavy band on underside of front wing. It is fast-flying and can be seen May/July on flowery mountain slopes from 600 to 1200m. The larva is like that of *machaon*, feeding on fennel and other umbellifers May/September. Confined to the islands of Corsica and Sardinia.

1. Black-veined White *Aporia crataegi*
Prominent black veins readily identify this
species, but female is thinly scaled and her
wings appear brownish and almost transparent. It flies rather weakly in open
country May/July, and large numbers may
gather to drink from wet ground. The larva
(1a) hibernates in communal webs while
very small, and feeds on trees and shrubs in
spring. C. & S. Europe; extinct in B.

2. Spanish Festoon *Zerynthia rumina*
This pretty and rather variable butterfly
flits daintily over rocky slopes, especially
coastal hills, February/May. Larva feeds on
birthworts in spring and summer. S.W.
Europe. Overlaps with **4** in S. France.

3. Apollo *Parnassius apollo*
This striking insect lives on mountain slopes between 800 and 2000m. There are several races, differing slightly in colour, but all have large eye-spots on the hind wing. Active July/August, they seem to float through the air, but only in bright sunlight. They spend much time sun-bathing on the ground. The dark, furry larva feeds on stonecrops and house-leeks in autumn and again in spring after hibernation. Most European mountains: not B.

4. Southern Festoon *Zerynthia polyxena*
Very similar to **2**, but without red spots in basal half of upper side of front wing. April/May in rough, stony places. Larva feeds on birthworts. S.E. Europe.

4

1. **Large White** *Pieris brassicae*

This common insect flies April/September in flowery places, especially near cultivation. There are two or three broods, summer insects having blacker wing tips than spring ones. Female has black spots on upper side of front wing as well as below. Eggs are laid in batches on brassicas and the larvae **(1a)** feed gregariously in summer and autumn. All Europe: much migration into Britain each spring, leading to very high populations in the summer.

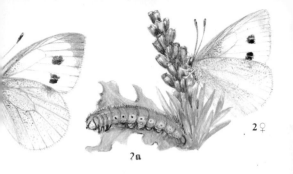

2♀

2a

2♂

3

2. Small White *Artogeia rapae*

Smaller and daintier than **1**, this species flies in gardens and other flowery places March/October in two or more broods. Spring insects have paler markings. Female has two black spots on upper side of front wing, but male has only one or even none. Eggs are laid singly on brassicas and larvae (**2a**) feed April/October. Most Europe. (*P. mannii* of S. Europe very similar, but wing tip markings larger.)

3. Green-veined White *Artogeia napi*

Flying March/October, this insect is easily identified by the green veins on underside. Female normally has two spots on upper side of front wing. Less of a pest than **1** and **2**, the green larva feeds on charlock and similar weeds April/October. All Europe.

1. Bath White *Pontia daplidice*

This fast-flying insect inhabits flowery places February/October, with two or three broods. Markings are often paler and less extensive in summer insects (**1a**). Always a solitary white spot in cell on underside of hind wing. Female has extra black spot near hind edge of upper side of front wing. The larva, bluish-grey with yellow stripes, eats mignonette and various crucifers March/July. S. & C. Europe: rare visitor to B.

2. Morocco Orange-tip *Anthocaris belia*

This swift little butterfly flies May/July in hilly districts. Female is white on upper side with a narrow orange tip, and yellow and white below. The larva feeds on buckler mustard during the summer. S. Europe.

1a

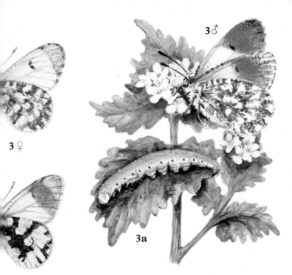

3♂

3♀

3a

3. Orange Tip *Anthocaris cardamines*

This delicate butterfly flies over flowery roadsides, meadows, and woodland glades April/June. Female lacks orange tips. The butterfly normally rests with wings closed, and is then hard to see among the vegetation. The slender green larva (**3a**) feeds May/July on the developing seed pods of cuckooflower, honesty, garlic mustard, and other crucifers. Most Europe.

1

2 ♂

2a ♀

1. Berger's Clouded Yellow
Colias australis
Two or three broods fly over rough ground May/September. Female has similar markings on a pale greenish-white background. The larva, blue-green and marked with yellow lines and black spots, feeds on horseshoe vetch in summer. S. & C. Europe, occasionally visiting B. (See also **4**.)

2. Clouded Yellow *Colias crocea*
This strong-flying insect flies in open country April/October. Female is paler, with yellow spots in the marginal bands. Some females are very pale and known as form *helice* (**2a**): broad margins distinguish them from female **4**. The larva, green with a yellow stripe on each side, eats clovers and related plants May/October. S. & C. Europe: summer visitor to B.

3

3. Mountain Clouded Yellow
Colias phicomone
The male upper side is very pale yellow, heavily dusted with dark grey. Female is greenish-white with much less grey. It flies June/September on grassy mountain slopes above 2000m. The larva feeds on vetches July/October. Alps & Pyrenees.

4. Pale Clouded Yellow *Colias hyale*
Two broods fly May/Setember in flowery fields up to 2000m. Female marked like male, but her ground colour is almost white on the upper side. Male distinguished from **1** by paler yellow and slightly more pointed wing tips. The larva, green with a yellow stripe on each side, feeds on lucerne and other leguminous plants June/October. S. & C. Europe: sporadic summer visitor to B.

4

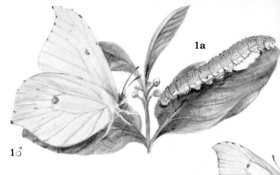

1a

1♂

1. **Brimstone** *Gonepteryx rhamni*

Male is brilliant yellow above, while female is greenish-white and easily mistaken for a large white in flight. Flies strongly around gardens, hedgerows, and woodland glades June/September and then goes into hibernation and appears again early in spring. The larva **(1a)** feeds on buckthorns May/June. Most Europe.

1 ♀

2. **Cleopatra** *Gonepteryx cleopatra*

Male is distinguished from **1** by orange flush on front wing and by the much paler underside. Female is like female brimstone but has less green on it. It flies in light woodland, especially in hilly areas, May/August and again in early spring after hibernation. The larva feeds on buckthorns May/September. S. Europe.

2

white below
tip ▽

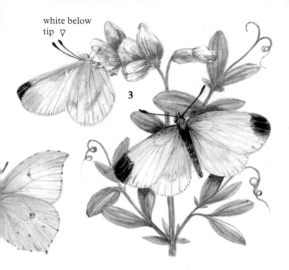

3. Wood White *Leptidea sinapis*

This flimsy-winged insect flutters weakly in light woodland May/August, with two or more broods. First brood is very grey below and has much paler patch on wing tip. Females never have much wing-tip marking. The narrow green larva eats vetches and other leguminous plants May/September. Most Europe. (*L. duponcheli* of S. Europe is similar, but antenna lacks white below tip.)

1. Nettle-tree Butterfly *Libythea celtis*
Easily recognised by the tooth on front
wing, this species flies June/September and
again March/April after hibernation. It
inhabits rough and cultivated land up to
1500m. The larva feeds on the nettle tree
April/June. S. Europe.

2a

2. Map Butterfly *Araschnia levana*
This butterfly inhabits wooded areas and
rough country up to 3000m. It flies April/
June and August/September. Spring insects (**2a**) are brighter and smaller than
summer ones (**2b**), and could be taken for
different species. The spiny black larvae
feed gregariously on stinging nettles May/
September. C. Europe, from France eastwards.

2b

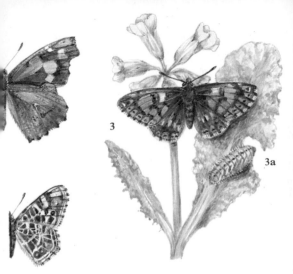

3. Duke of Burgundy Fritillary

Hamearis lucina

Not a true fritillary, this attractive butterfly inhabits woodland clearings and sheltered, grassy hillsides. On the wing May/June (and again in August in S. Europe), it is a restless insect, flitting rapidly from plant to plant and rarely settling for long. Often settles on ground. The larva **(3a)** feeds on cowslips and primroses June/July. Most Europe, but not north.

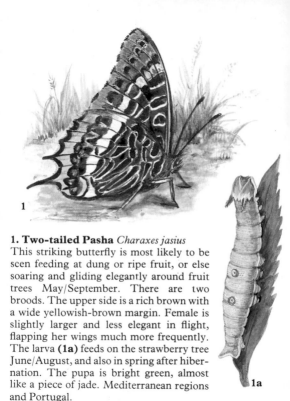

1. Two-tailed Pasha *Charaxes jasius*
This striking butterfly is most likely to be seen feeding at dung or ripe fruit, or else soaring and gliding elegantly around fruit trees May/September. There are two broods. The upper side is a rich brown with a wide yellowish-brown margin. Female is slightly larger and less elegant in flight, flapping her wings much more frequently. The larva **(1a)** feeds on the strawberry tree June/August, and also in spring after hibernation. The pupa is bright green, almost like a piece of jade. Mediterranean regions and Portugal.

34

2. Monarch *Danaus plexippus*

Also known as the milkweed, this beautiful butterfly is a native of the Americas and the Pacific region to Australia and S.E. Asia. It also breeds in the Canary Islands. It is a strong-flying species with marked migratory habits, and occasional specimens turn up on the coasts of western Europe in summer. The species cannot breed here, for the milkweeds (*Asclepias*) on which the larvae **(2a)** feed do not grow here. Sexes are alike, but female somewhat paler.

1. Purple Emperor *Apatura iris*

This fine insect flies July/August in mature woodlands, especially where oak is common. Male has a brilliant purple sheen when seen from certain angles. He keeps mainly to the tree tops, but comes down to feed at bramble blossoms and is also attracted to muddy pools and carrion. Female is larger, with larger white markings but no purple sheen. The larva **(1a)** feeds on sallow August/September and again May/June after hibernation. C. Europe from S. England eastwards.

2. Lesser Purple Emperor *Apatura ilia*
Distinguished from **1** by the prominent eye-spot near middle of front wing, this butterfly inhabits lightly wooded hills May/September. There are two broods in southern areas. Female is larger, without purple flush. Both sexes also exist in a form in which most of pale markings on upper side are yellowish brown. Larvae eat willows and poplars in the spring and early summer and before autumn hibernation. C. & S. Europe: not B.

1. White Admiral *Limenitis camilla*

This woodland insect can be seen feeding at bramble flowers or gliding swiftly just above head height in rides and glades June/August. It also likes to sunbathe with wings open on foliage, where its black and white pattern blends amazingly well with dappled sunlight. The underside resembles **3**, but with less white. The larva **(1a)** eats honeysuckle, hibernating between two leaves while still small and completing growth May/June. Most Europe: southern B. only.

2

2. Poplar Admiral *Limenitis populi*

This strong-flying butterfly occurs in and around open woodland June/July. Female has larger white markings. Underside is not unlike paler version of **3**, with less white. The larva feeds on poplars, hibernating while small and completing growth in spring. Most Europe: not B.

3. Southern White Admiral
Limenitis reducta

The prominent white spot in middle of front wing distinguishes this species from **1**. It glides elegantly in light woodland and scrub May/October, with one, two, or three broods. The larvae eat honeysuckle in summer: those hatching in autumn hibernate like **1**. S & C. Europe: not B.

3

1. Small Tortoiseshell *Aglais urticae*
This common garden butterfly comes out to feed and sunbathe on spring flowers as early as February in some years. A new generation flies in flowery places from May onwards and a second brood generally flies in late summer before going into hibernation. There is only one brood in the north. The spiky, black and green larvae feed on stinging nettles in spring and summer, spending their early lives in communal webs of silk. All Europe.

2. Hungarian Glider *Neptis rivularis*
This dainty butterfly glides and floats through light woodland June/July, reaching altitudes of 1000m. The larva feeds on spiraea and possibly meadowsweet July/August. From Switzerland eastwards.

3. Large Tortoiseshell
Nymphalis polychloros
Distinguished from **1** by its larger size and less distinct black area at base of hind wing, the large tortoiseshell flies in lightly wooded areas June/August and again in spring after hibernation. Batches of eggs are laid on twigs of elm, sallow, and other trees in spring, and the larvae **(3a)** feed gregariously in silken nests when the leaves open. Most Europe: S.E. England only.

1. Camberwell Beauty
Nymphalis antiopa

This insect flies strongly in lightly wooded country, especially in hilly areas, June/August and again after hibernation in spring. It is attracted to oozing sap and ripe fruit. Underside similar to upper, but lacks blue spots. Cream borders fade during hibernation. Female larger. The larva **(1a)** feeds gregariously on willows in spring. Most Europe: rare visitor to eastern B.

1a

2. Peacock *Inachis io*

This unmistakable species is commonly seen in gardens and other flowery places July/September. It is very fond of buddleia and other garden flowers, usually feeding with wings wide open. The insect hibernates in hollow trees and out-houses, where the almost black underside camouflages it very well, and flies again in spring – by which time it is often torn and faded. The larva **(2a)** feeds on stinging nettles May/July. All Europe except far north.

1. Red Admiral *Vanessa atalanta*

This striking insect flies in gardens and other flowery places May/October, but is not common in N. & C. Europe until August. Adults hibernate in S. Europe and many fly north in spring. It is their progeny that are common on flowers and ripe fruit in autumn. Probably none survives the northern winter. The larva **(1a)** feeds on stinging nettle and thistle. Most Europe.

2. **Painted Lady** *Cynthia cardui*

This strong-flying, migratory species has a similar life history to **1**, and arrives in B. from Africa and S. Europe in June. A new generation flies in flowery places August/September, but none survives the northern winter. Some fly south in autumn. The dark, spiny larvae eat thistles and burdock June/August. All Europe.

3. **Comma** *Polygonia c-album*

Named for the comma-like mark on underside, the comma inhabits woods, gardens, and hedgerows. One brood, with paler colours, flies June/July, and a second flies August/October before hibernating and re-appearing in spring. The larva, resembling a bird-dropping, feeds on nettle, hop, and elm. Most Europe: southern B. only.

1 ♀

1 ♂

1. Silver-washed Fritillary
Argynnis paphia
Bands of silvery scales on the underside give this handsome species its name. Female is larger; male has smaller spots, and prominent streaks on veins. Female also occurs in a very dark form called *valezina*. It flies June/August in wooded areas. The spiky, brownish larva hibernates as soon as it leaves the egg and feeds on violets April/June. Most Europe.

2. Cardinal *Pandoriana pandora*
The paler green and the prominent brick-red area on underside of front wing distinguish this species from **1**. It is also greener on upper side than **1**. The insect flies June/July in flowery meadows and the larva feeds on violets. S. Europe.

3. High Brown Fritillary

Fabriciana adippe

One of several similar species, this can usually be distinguished by the row of silver-pupilled spots beyond centre of underside of hind wing. Like **1** and **2**, it is a strong flier and can be seen in woodland glades and flowery meadows June/July. The larva remains in the egg for the winter and hatches to feed on violets April/June. Most Europe.

47

1. Queen of Spain Fritillary

Issoria lathonia

This beautiful fritillary is easily recognised by the large silvery spots on underside. It flies strongly over rough ground and flowery meadows February onwards, with up to three broods. It enjoys sunbathing with wings open. The larva feeds on violets throughout the summer. Most Europe, with much northward migration in spring: only occasional visitor to B.

2. Dark Green Fritillary
Mesoacidalia aglaja
The underside of this butterfly is thickly dusted with green, and all hind wing spots are silver. Female has slightly paler ground colour and heavier markings. The insect flies strongly over rough hillsides and other flowery places June/August. The larva, velvety black with red spots, feeds on violets in spring. All Europe.

3. Marbled Fritillary *Brenthis daphne*
This brightly coloured species can be recognised by the marked rounding of hind wings and also by the fairly well defined purplish band on underside of hind wings. Female is slightly larger and paler on upper side. The insect haunts sheltered valleys and hillsides June/July and feeds at bramble flowers. The larva feeds on violets and bramble in spring. S. Europe.

49

1. Heath Fritillary *Mellicta athalia*
This species flies May/September in woodland glades and flowery meadows. Flight is weak and the insect takes frequent rests on the herbage. The amount of dark pattern varies enormously, making identification difficult. The dark brown larva feeds on cow-wheat and plantain in late summer and again after hibernation in spring. All Europe, but v. rare in B. (south only).

2. False Heath Fritillary
Melitaea diamina
This species resembles **1**, but is generally more heavily marked with brown. Orange lunules on underside of hind wing enclose small spots, and marginal line on underside is orange/yellow. It flies May/July in grassy meadows. The larva feeds mainly on plantains in summer. Most Europe. Not B.

3. Pearl-bordered Fritillary

Clossiana euphrosyne

Inhabiting light woodland, this fast-flying insect keeps close to the ground as it searches for flowers April/August. It is distinguished from **4** by the bright silver marginal spots on underside of hind wing and by the large silver spot in centre. The larva (**3a**) feeds on violets in summer and again in spring. All Europe.

4. Small Pearl-bordered Fritillary

Clossiana selene

Very similar to **3**, this insect is distinguished by central band on underside of hind wing being all silver or all yellow. The marginal spots may also be yellow. Its habits are like those of **3**, but it tends to fly a little later. The larva is much paler than that of **3**. All Europe except far south.

1. Knapweed Fritillary *Melitaea phoebe*
This insect is generally heavily marked with
brown on upper side. The well-marked yel-
low sub-marginal band on underside of hind
wing has a round red spot in each space.
Female larger. It flies in flowery places
April/September, with up to three broods.
The larvae eat knapweeds and plantains.
S. & C. Europe: not B.

2. Niobe Fritillary *Fabriciana niobe*
A small white spot in cell of underside of
hind wing, together with black-edged veins
on underside, distinguishes this insect from
the high brown fritillary (p.47). Female often
greyish with heavier markings. It flies in
meadows June//July. The larva eats violets
and plantains. Most Europe: not B.

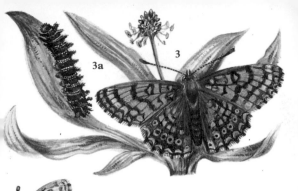

3. Glanville Fritillary *Melitaea cinxia*

This slow-flying, ground-hugging insect inhabits flowery meadows May/September, with one or two broods. Upper side of hind wing has four or five round black sub-marginal spots. Female often larger. The larva **(3a)** feeds on plantains, hibernating while small and feeding up in spring. Most Europe: (Isle of Wight only in B.).

4. Violet Fritillary *Clossiana dia*

This dainty butterfly flits nimbly through lightly wooded, hilly areas April/September, with two or three broods. It is easily recognised by its small size and the violet-brown coloration of hind wing underside. The larva feeds on violets and other low-growing plants. S. & C. Europe: not B.

1a

1. Spotted Fritillary *Melitaea didyma*

This widely distributed butterfly is very variable. It flies May/September with up to three broods, inhabiting flowery meadows and rough ground up to 2000m. The typical form of C. Europe **(1a)** is bright tawny red with irregular dark markings. Underside of hind wing is basically cream with two orange bands, and the marginal spots are always distinctly rounded. Female is larger and paler. In mountain areas the insect exists in the form known as *meridionalis*: male is quite like the lowland form, although a little larger, but female **(1b)** is heavily dusted with grey. In S. Europe the insect is very bright with small spots (form *occidentalis*). All forms grade into each other, and there is a good deal of variation between broods, but underside of hind wing always retains its basic pattern. The larva feeds on plantains and toadflax. S. & C. Europe: not B.

1b

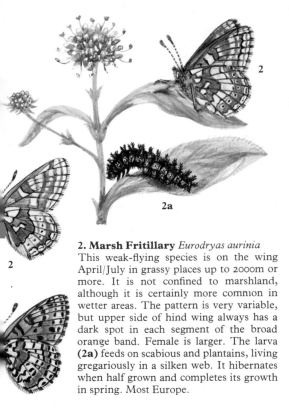

2

2a

2

2. Marsh Fritillary *Eurodryas aurinia*
This weak-flying species is on the wing
April/July in grassy places up to 2000m or
more. It is not confined to marshland,
although it is certainly more common in
wetter areas. The pattern is very variable,
but upper side of hind wing always has a
dark spot in each segment of the broad
orange band. Female is larger. The larva
(2a) feeds on scabious and plantains, living
gregariously in a silken web. It hibernates
when half grown and completes its growth
in spring. Most Europe.

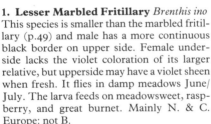

1. Lesser Marbled Fritillary *Brenthis ino*
This species is smaller than the marbled fritillary (p.49) and male has a more continuous black border on upper side. Female underside lacks the violet coloration of its larger relative, but upperside may have a violet sheen when fresh. It flies in damp meadows June/July. The larva feeds on meadowsweet, raspberry, and great burnet. Mainly N. & C. Europe: not B.

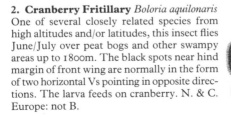

2. Cranberry Fritillary *Boloria aquilonaris*
One of several closely related species from high altitudes and/or latitudes, this insect flies June/July over peat bogs and other swampy areas up to 1800m. The black spots near hind margin of front wing are normally in the form of two horizontal Vs pointing in opposite directions. The larva feeds on cranberry. N. & C. Europe: not B.

3♀

3♂

3. Idas Blue *Lycaeides idas*

4♂

Flying May/August, with one brood in the north and two in the south, this species inhabits rough ground up to 1200m. Male has relatively narrow black borders on upperside. Underside of hind wing has metallic blue pupils in black spots near outer angle. Female is largely brown above. The larva eats various leguminous plants and spends its later life in ants' nests like the large blue (p.60). Most Europe: not B.

4. Cranberry Blue *Vacciniina optilete*

4♀

Male has deep violet-blue upperside with narrow black margins. Both sexes have *red* spots near angle of underside of hind wing. It flies July over moorland and mountain slopes to 2100m. The larva eats cranberry and related plants. N. & E. from Alps.

1♀

1♂

1. Long-tailed Blue *Lampides boeticus*

This strongly migratory butterfly occurs in nearly all the warmer parts of the world. In Europe, it flies throughout the summer in rough flowery places up to 2000m. There are two or three broods. Hindwing is distinctly tailed and male has rather hairy violet-blue upperside. Female has much broader borders on front wing. The larvae feed on the seed pods of various legumes. Resident in S. Europe, spreading northwards during summer: rare visitor to B.

2♀

2. Lang's Short-tailed Blue

Syntarucus pirithous

An inhabitant of flowery places, usually at low altitudes, this butterfly flies in spring and summer. Male has violet-blue upper side with few black marks: underside is like that of female. The larvae feed on various leguminous plants. S. Europe, especially near the coasts.

3

3. Little Blue *Cupido minimus*

Among the smallest of European butterflies, this species flies May/September in grassy places, usually on chalk or limestone. Both sexes are brown on upperside, but male has a dusting of blue scales. The larva is brownish, sometimes tinged with pink, and feeds on the flowers and seed heads of leguminous plants in summer. Most Europe.

4. Short-tailed Blue *Everes argiades*

This little butterfly flies in flowery places from April onwards, with two or more broods. Male of first brood is violet-blue with narrow black borders: later insects are often larger and darker. Female is black with blue flush at base (reduced or absent in summer insects) and generally an orange spot at corner of hind wing. The larva feeds on trefoils and other leguminous plants. S. & C. Europe: rare visitor to B.

4

1. **Large Blue** *Maculinea arion*

This interesting species flies June/July in rough, grassy places up to 2000m. Both sexes are bright blue, but male has smaller black markings than female. Underside alike in both sexes. The larvae feed on wild thyme at first, but then wander about until they are picked up by ants and taken into the ants' nests. Here they are fed on small ant larvae, and in return they exude a sweet fluid for the ants. The caterpillars hibernate in the nest before pupating in spring. Most Europe: recently declared extinct in B.

2. **Green-underside Blue**
Glaucopsyche alexis

An insect of flowery hillsides, this species flies April/July. Female is brown with blue flush at base. The larvae feed on small legumes. Most Europe: not B.

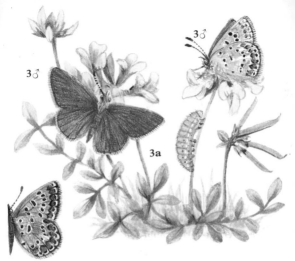

3♂

3♂

3a

3♀

3. Common Blue *Polyommatus icarus*
This, the commonest of the European blues, flies April onwards in all kinds of grassy country up to 2000m. Male has a violet-blue upperside with narrow black margins, while underside usually has a white stripe in centre of hind wing. Female is brown, with a variable amount of blue at base of wings. The underside markings are stronger than in male. The larva **(3a)** feeds on trefoils and other legumes. All Europe.

1. Chalkhill Blue *Lysandra coridon*

This species flies July/August in chalk and limestone districts up to 2000m. Female is brown, often with a dusting of blue near base of wings. Underside is grey in male, brown in female, and marked like Common Blue, although orange spots are less prominent. The larvae feed on horseshoe vetch and other legumes and hibernate while small. S. & C. Europe: southern B only.

2. Damon Blue *Agrodiaetus damon*

The underside, with its prominent white stripe and no orange spots, distinguishes this species from other blues. Female is brown above, often with a dusting of blue, and coffee-coloured below, marked like male. It flies July/August in hilly limestone regions. The larva feeds on sainfoin. Mountains of S. & C. Europe: not B.

3 ♀

3. Holly Blue *Celastrina argiolus*

A common insect of light woodland, gardens, and hedgerows, the holly blue flies April/May and again July/August. Male is shining blue with much narrower black edges than female. Second-brood females are darker with even broader black borders. Spring larvae feed on the flower buds of holly: autumn ones eat ivy buds. Most Europe.

4. Mazarine Blue *Cyaniris semiargus*

This butterfly frequents flowery meadows and hillsides to 1800m. Scores of individuals often congregate to drink from muddy pools and damp ground. Male is deep violet-blue, while female is uniformly brown above. Underside of female is brown, but marked like male. Larva feeds on legumes and other low-growing plants and hibernates while small. Most Europe: not B.

4

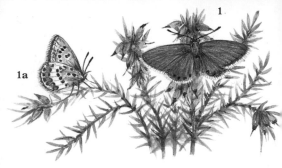

1. Silver-studded Blue *Plebejus argus*
This heathland insect gets its name from the sub-marginal spots on underside of hind wing (**1a**): each black spot has a shiny centre. Female is brown and resembles **2**, but there is often some blue near body and the orange spots may be absent. It flies May/ August. The larva feeds on the flowers of heather, gorse, and other plants. Most Europe: southern B. only.

2. Brown Argus *Aricia agestis*
Although there is no trace of blue in either sex, this insect is clearly a 'blue' from the underside pattern. The orange spots on upperside are often reduced, especially on front wing. It flies in heathy and grassy places April onwards. The larva feeds on rockrose, storksbill, and other plants. S. & C. Europe.

2

3a

3♂

3♀

3. Adonis Blue *Lysandra bellargus*

The male is the most vivid of all the blues, much purer in colour than most of its relatives. Underside **(3a)** often has a blue flush near base. Female is brown, often with a blue haze at base: underside is browner than male with little or no blue. Both sexes have a distinctly chequered border. It flies May/June and again July/August on chalk and limestone grasslands. The larva feeds on horseshoe vetch and other legumes. S. & C. Europe: southern B only.

1a

1b

1. Green Hairstreak *Callophrys rubi*

The uniform brown upperside (**1a**) and leaf-green underside (**1b**) make this species instantly recognisable, although the alternate flashing of brown and green make it difficult to follow as it flits about in rough, grassy places March/July. The white dots on the underside are sometimes absent, especially from front wing. The larvae is pale green and feeds on broom, gorse, heather, and various other shrubby plants in summer. All Europe.

2 ♀

2. Black Hairstreak *Strymonidia pruni*

This butterfly flies May/July in light woodland and scrub with blackthorn bushes. Male is similar to female but lacks pale flush on front wing. The larva is green with purple ridges and feeds on blackthorn in spring. Most Europe: very rare in B.

3 ♀

3. Brown Hairstreak *Thecla betulae*

This species flies in light woodland July/
September. Male lacks orange flash on
front wing, although there may be a small
patch. Underside is brick-coloured with
white lines – the 'hair streaks'. The larva is
pale green and feeds on blackthorn May/
June. Most Europe: southern B only.

4. White-letter Hairstreak
Strymonida w-album

This species gets its name from the w-shaped
mark formed by the white streak on underside of hind wing. It is like a male **2**, but
never has marginal spots on underside of
front wing. It flies along woodland margins
July/August and is very fond of bramble
blossom. The larvae is yellowish green with
a black head and feeds on elm May/June.
Most Europe: southern B only.

1♂   ♀

1. **Blue-spot Hairstreak** *Strymonidia spini*

This species is common June/July in scrubby places, especially in hills. The blue spot on underside of hind wing **(1a)** distinguishes it from **2** and other similar hairstreaks. Male has a small oval scent brand on front wing. Female is larger and more strongly marked below. In S.W. Europe female often has orange patches **(1b)**. The larvae feed on blackthorn and other shrubs. S. & C. Europe: not B.

2. **Ilex Hairstreak** *Nordmannia ilicis*

This species flies June/July on rough ground with scrubby oaks on which the larvae feed. The red markings on underside are larger in female. Both sexes may have an orange patch on front wing. S. & C. Europe: not B.

3. **Purple Hairstreak** *Quercusia quercus*

This woodland butterfly is most likely to be seen flying round tall oaks July/August, although it sometimes descends to feed at bramble blossom. Male has gleaming purple on both wings, but female has just a bright patch on front wing. Underside **(3a)** is similar in both sexes, but female may be more boldly marked. The larva is reddish brown and feeds on oak May/June. Most Europe except far north.

4. **Provence Hairstreak** *Tomares ballus*

This little butterfly flits over rough, stony ground in early spring. Male lacks the bright orange on upperside, although it may have small orange spots at corner of hind wing. Undersides are alike in both sexes. The larvae feed on low-growing leguminous plants. Iberia & S. France.

4♀

1 ♀

2

3

1. Large Copper *Lycaena dispar*
This beautiful insect flies in fens and other damp places May/September. Male lacks most of the dark colouring and resembles **2**. Underside of hind wing is grey with black and orange markings. The larva feeds on docks. Scattered in S. & C. Europe: maintained artificially in B.

2. Scarce Copper *Heodes virgaureae*
The yellowish underside with white marks distinguishes this insect from other coppers. Female is heavily marked with brown on upper side. It flies in flowery places, especially in hills, July/August. The larva eats docks. Most Europe: not B.

3. Sooty Copper *Heodes tityrus*
This well-named species flies April/September in flowery meadows. Female has orange and more rounded front wings with the typical pattern of black dots. The larvae feed on docks. S. & C. Europe: not B.

4

4. Small Copper *Lycaena phlaeas*

This species abounds March/October in grassy places up to 2000m. Underside of front wing resembles **2**, but hind wing is greyish brown with obscure markings. The larva is green with a dark head and eats docks and sorrels. All Europe.

5. Purple-edged Copper

Palaeochrysophanus hippothöe

This species flies June/August in damp meadows and bogs, especially in the mountains. Front wings of male are edged with purple on front. Female is much browner. Larvae feed on docks. Most Europe: not B.

6. Purple-shot Copper *Heodes alciphron*

Male is distinguished from **5** by the violet sheen almost all over wings, although the violet is reduced in the mountains of S. Europe. Female is largely brown with an irregular row of darker spots on front wing. It flies June/August in flowery places. The larva eats docks. S. & C. Europe: not B.

5

6

1. Marbled White *Melanargia galathea*

Despite its name, this butterfly is a 'brown', as can be seen by the marginal eye-spots. Upperside is chequered black and white. Female is larger, with yellowish brown markings on underside of hind wing. It flies with a strong, flapping flight over rough grassy places July/August. The larva **(1a)** hibernates soon after hatching and feeds on various grasses in spring. S. & C. Europe: southern B only.

2. Western Marbled White
Melanargia occitanica

This species differ from **1** in having a black bar across the cell of front wing. Veins of underside are brown. It flies May/July in dry, rocky places to 1800m. The larva is like that of **1**. S. & S.W. Europe.

3. Woodland Grayling *Hipparchia fagi*
One of several similar species, this insect
inhabits scrub and light woodland July/
August. Upper side is dull brown with a
broad pale band – very like underside but
hind wing is not mottled. Female is larger,
with paler band on upperside and two eye-
spots on front wing: male has only one. The
larva feeds on grasses and hibernates when
part-grown. S. & C. Europe: not B.

4. Tree Grayling *Neohipparchia statilinus*
This insect flies in dry, scrubby places and
sparse woodland July/September. Female
is pale on upperside, especially in outer
third of wing, and markings are more obvious; underside often much greyer. The
larva feeds on grasses and hibernates when
part grown. S. & C. Europe: not B.

1. Grayling *Hipparchia semele*

This strong-flying butterfly flies on heathland and dry grassland July/August. Its mottled underside **(1a)** provides fine camouflage. Male normally has smaller pale patches than female and also has a dark scent band on front wing. The larva **(1b)** feeds on grasses, hibernating when young and completing its growth in spring. All Europe except far north and south.

2. Baltic Grayling *Oeneis jutta*

This insect flies May/July among pines and over lowland bogs. It can be recognised by the two or three blind (without white centre) ocelli ringed with yellow on front wing. Female is larger and has larger yellow patches around ocelli, often linked into a broad band. Larvae eat grass. Scandinavia.

2

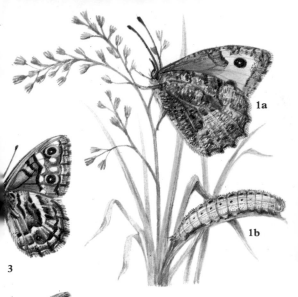

3. Striped Grayling *Pseudotergumia fidia*

The black and white striped underside and the white spots on upper side distinguish this species from most other graylings. Female is larger, usually paler, and with larger and bolder markings on upper side. Larvae feed on grasses. Adults fly July/August in rocky areas to 2000m. S.W. Europe.

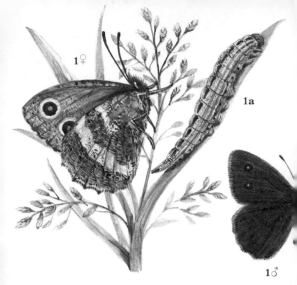

1 ♀

1a

1 ♂

1. The Dryad *Minois dryas*

This species flies July/August in grassy places and light woodland and can be distinguished from most other browns by the blue-pupilled ocelli. The latter are much larger in female than in male. The adults are fond of lavender flowers on rough hillsides in southern Europe, while the larva **(1a)** feeds on various grasses. S. & C. Europe: not B.

2. Great Banded Grayling *Brintesia circe*

An inhabitant of light woodland and rough hillsides, this handsome butterfly flies June/July. It glides rather lazily, very much like a white admiral, and spends much time on the ground, often settling on roads in large numbers. Female is similar, but larger. Underside is paler and mottled, but still with broad pale bands. The larvae feed on various grasses. S. & C. Europe: not B.

3. The Hermit *Chazara briseis*

This insect flies over rough, dry hillsides and plateaux from June until late summer. It can fly rapidly, but rarely flies far and spends much time on the stony ground. Female is larger and with less distinct markings on underside of hind wing. The larva feeds on grasses. S & C. Europe: not B.

1. The Scotch Argus *Erebia aethiops*
One of many very similar *Erebia* species, most of which fly in the mountains, this insect flies August/September on moors and in damp coniferous forests up to 2000m. Underside of front wing is similar to upperside, but hind wing has pale bands and lacks prominent ocelli. The female is paler. The larva, brown with darker stripes, feeds on grasses in autumn and spring. C. Europe: northern B. only.

2. Mountain Ringlet *Erebia epiphron*
This insect flies June/August on moors and mountain grasslands. There are numerous sub-species, in which the brick-coloured bands are often reduced or even absent. The larvae feed on grasses in summer. S. & C. Europe: northern B only.

3

3a

3. **Ringlet** *Aphantopus hyperantus*
Easily recognised by the large ocelli on underside, the ringlet flies June/August in light woodland, hedgerows, and damp grassland. Female is paler. Upperside is ± uniform brown with indistinct eye-spots. The larva (**3a**) feeds on grasses before and after hibernation. Most Europe.

4. **Arran Brown** *Erebia ligia*
Despite its name, the existence of this butterfly on the Isle of Arran has never been confirmed. It is distinguished from **1** by the white stripe on underside of hind wing, although this runs only half way back in female. It flies June/August on moorland and in light woodland up to 1500m. The larva feeds on grasses. C. & N. Europe: doubtful in B.

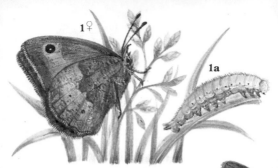

1. Meadow Brown *Maniola jurtina*

One of Europe's commonest butterflies, the
meadow brown flies June/August in all
kinds of grassy places up to 2000m. Upperside of male is ± uniform dull brown, but
female has pale patches on front wing.
Female is more boldly marked on underside
but lacks the small black spots on hind
wing. The larva **(1a)** feeds on grasses. All
Europe except far north.

2. Dusky Meadow Brown
Hyponephele lycaon

This species can be distinguished from **1**
by the wavy margin of the hind wing.
Female is also distinguished by having two
equal-sized ocelli on front wing. It flies
July/August in dry, rocky places. The larva
eats grasses. Most Europe except NW:
not B.

3. Woodland Ringlet *Erebia medusa*
The underside of this butterfly is almost identical to the upperside, thus distinguishing the species from the very similar Scotch argus and Arran brown. Female is slightly paler and larger. The insect flies May/June on moorlands and damp grassland, and also in light woodland up to 1500m. The larvae eat grasses. C. Europe: not B.

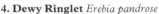

4. Dewy Ringlet *Erebia pandrose*
This butterfly flies June/July over rough slopes and meadows. Only above 2000m in south, but much lower down in the north. The greyish underside of hind wing with its two dark bands distinguishes it from most other *Erebia* species. Female is similar, but paler. The larvae feed on grasses. N. Scandinavia and mountains of S. Europe.

4

1. Large Heath *Coenonympha tullia*
This widespread insect has several sub-species, varying in density of colour and development of ocelli on underside. Ocelli are absent in *C.t.scotica* of N. Scotland – one of three sub-species in Britain. Upper-side never has a dark border. Female is often paler. It flies June/July over upland and lowland moors, but only in mountains in S.E. Europe. The greenish larvae eat cotton-grass and other sedges before and after hibernation. Most Europe except S.W.

1♀

2. Dusky Heath *Coenonympha dorus*
This butterfly flies June/July in dry, stony places up to 1800m. It may lack ocelli on both surfaces of hind wing. Female much more orange on front wing. Larval food plant unknown. S.W. Europe.

2

3. Small Heath *Coenonympha pamphilus*
This insect flies throughout summer and frequents all kinds of grassy and heathy places. The ocelli on underside of hind wing vary in development and may be absent in north. The larva, clear green with dark stripes, feeds on grasses. Larvae hatching May/June may mature in summer, but some hibernate and complete their growth in spring. Larvae hatching late summer all hibernate. All Europe.

1. Woodland Brown *Lopinga achine*

This very local butterfly flies June/July in shady woodlands up to 1000m. The upperside is uniform brown with large yellow-ringed, blind ocelli. Female is paler and slightly larger. The larvae eat grasses. N. & C. Europe: not B.

2. Large Wall Brown *Lasiommata maera*

This butterfly flies May/September in one or two broods and inhabits rough grassy places up to 2000m. The female lacks the dark scent brand in middle of front wing and has much brighter orange patches round ocelli. Both sexes are much brighter and more orange in south-western parts of range and are then similar to **3**, but they are distinguished by having only a single dark bar in cell of front wing. There may be one or two pupils in main ocellus. The larvae feed on grasses. Most Europe: not B.

3. Wall Brown *Lasiommata megera*　△

Two or three broods of this very common insect fly over roadsides and rough grasslands from March until autumn. It likes to sunbathe on rocks and walls. Two bars in cell of front wing distinguish it from **2**. Female is paler and lacks the scent brand in centre of front wing. Underside is like **4**, but with more orange on front wing. The larvae, green with white dots, eat grasses. Those hatching in late summer hibernate in autumn. Most Europe except far north.

4. Northern Wall Brown
Lasiommata petropolitana

This species resembles **2**, but is smaller. Male is more uniformly brown on both surfaces with less orange round the ocelli. It flies May/July in open coniferous woods up to 2000m. The larvae feed on grasses. Scandinavia and mountains of S. Europe.

4 ♀

85

1 ♀

1. Gatekeeper *Pyronia tithonus*

Also known as the hedge brown, this species frequents sunny woodland glades, hedgerows, and gardens July/August. It is very fond of bramble blossom. Female is larger than male and lacks scent brand on front wing. Underside of female is more yellow. The larva is greenish grey with a brown head and eats grasses August/September and again April/June after hibernation. S. & C. Europe. (Southern Gatekeeper (*P. cecilia*) has grey on underside of hind wing.)

1 ♂

2. Spanish Gatekeeper *Pyronia bathseba*

This species resembles **1**, but has more prominent ocelli on hind wing and a more clear cut discal stripe on underside..Female is larger. It flies May/August in rough grassy places and hedgerows. The larvae eat grasses. Iberia & S. France.

2

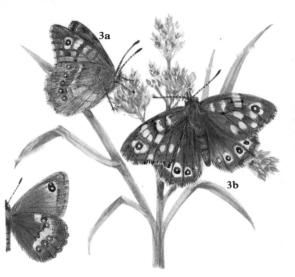

3. Speckled Wood *Pararge aegeria*

This attractive species flies March/October in woods and other shady places, often basking in dappled sunlight. There are two subspecies. *P. a. aegeria* (**3a**) has bright orange spots; *P. a. tircis* (**3b**) has creamy white markings. The wrinkled green larvae eat grasses. There are two or three broods, winter being passed as larvae or pupae. Most Europe: *aegeria* in S. & W., *tircis* in C. & N.

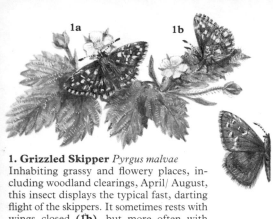

1. Grizzled Skipper *Pyrgus malvae*

Inhabiting grassy and flowery places, including woodland clearings, April/ August, this insect displays the typical fast, darting flight of the skippers. It sometimes rests with wings closed **(1b)**, but more often with them open **(1a)**. The wings have a distinct velvety texture. The larvae are green and brown and feed on cinquefoils, wild strawberry, and other low-growing plants. Most Europe: southern B. only.

2. Dingy skipper *Erynnis tages*

This insect flies May/June and sometimes later in flowery places up to 1800m, mostly on calcareous soils. It sunbathes on the ground or the vegetation with wings open, and rests at night in moth-like fashion with wings held roof-wise over the body. The larvae feed on birds-foot trefoil and other low-growing plants. Most Europe.

3♂

3♀

3. Large Grizzled Skipper *Pyrgus alveus*

Several sub-species live in Europe, some of them patterned very like **1**, but all can be distinguished from **1** by the larger size and the greenish yellow on underside of hind wing. Male is darker than female and has larger pale markings. It flies June/August in flowery meadows, most often between 1000 and 1800m. The larvae feed on rock-roses, cinquefoils, and other low-growing plants, especially members of the rose family. Most Europe: not B.

4. Red Underwing Skipper
Spialia sertorius

The brick-red colour on underside of hind wing gives this species its name. It is otherwise very similar to **1**. It flies April/August in rough grassy places up to 1500m. The larvae eat low-growing rosaceous plants, such as cinquefoil. S. & C. Europe: not B.

4

1. Large Skipper *Ochlodes venatus*

This insect darts rapidly about in flowery fields and other grassy places June/August. It may rest with wings half open (**1a**) or closed (**1b**). Female lacks dark scent brand in front wing and has a more mottled appearance. The larva is greenish and feeds on various grasses. It hibernates when half grown. Most Europe.

2. Small Skipper *Thymelicus sylvestris*

An inhabitant of rough, grassy and flowery places June/September, this insect behaves much like **1**. Female lacks the dark scent brand. The larva, pale green with a darker head, eats grasses in spring. Most Europe except north: southern B. only.

3. Silver-spotted Skipper *Hesperia comma*

The greenish underside with clear silvery markings easily distinguishes this species. Female lacks the scent brand in front wing. It flies July/August in grassy places on calcareous soils. The larvae feed on various grasses. Most Europe: southern B. only.

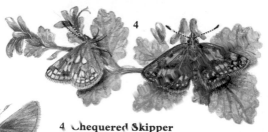

4

4 Chequered Skipper
Carterocephalus palaemon
This attractive butterfly flies June/July and usually haunts light woodlands and woodland glades, where it feeds on bugle and ground ivy flowers. Female is greyer on upperside, with paler markings. The larva feeds on grasses and, like most skipper larvae, forms a tubular retreat by fixing blades together with silk. It hibernates in such a retreat and completes its growth in spring. Most Europe except far south: very local; rare in B.

5. Large Chequered Skipper
Heteropterus morpheus
The bold pattern on underside of hind wing makes this an unmistakable insect. Female has larger pale markings on upperside and fringes are distinctly chequered black and white. It flies in woodland glades and other shady places June/July. The larva is pale grey or fawn and feeds on grasses. Scattered in S. & C. Europe (mostly eastern): not B.

5

1. **Lime Hawk** *Mimas tiliae*

Like most hawk-moths, this species flies rapidly and has narrow front wings. The ground colour varies from buff to brick-red. It flies May/July. The larva is hairless, like all hawk-moth larvae, and pale green with yellowish diagonal stripes. Like most hawk-moth larvae, it has a horn at the back. It feeds July/September, mainly on lime and elm. Most Europe: southern B. only.

2

2. Eyed Hawk *Smerinthus ocellata*

The eye-spots on hind wings are covered by front wings when at rest, but when disturbed the moth lifts front wings and displays the 'eyes'. Small birds are clearly frightened by this behaviour. It flies May/June and sometimes again in September. The larva, pale green with white dots and oblique stripes, feeds on sallow and apple June/September. Most Europe: not Scotland.

3. Poplar Hawk *Laothoe populi*

The front wings vary from pale grey to brown. The red spots on hind wings are hidden at rest, when the moth resembles a bunch of dead leaves, but they are exposed when the insect is disturbed. It flies May/June and August/September. The larva, bright green with yellow dots and stripes, feeds on poplars and sallows June/September. Most Europe.

1

1. Privet Hawk *Sphinx ligustri*
This, Britain's largest resident moth, flies June/July
and often rests on fences by day. The wings are
usually held back along the side of the body and the
insect looks like a piece of wood. It may be confused
with the convolvulus hawk, but the latter is greyer
and has no pink on hind wings. The larva, bright
green with purple and white diagonal stripes, feeds
on privet, ash, and lilac July/August. At rest, the
front end is raised and the head pulled in to resemble
a miniature sphinx. Most Europe: mainly southern
B.

2. **Pine Hawk** *Hyloicus pinastri*

This species inhabits pine forests and can be found by searching the trunks June/August, but it is hard to spot because its wings blend well with the bark on the lower parts of the trunk. The larva feeds on pine and spruce needles July/September. It is green with white stripes when young and it rests on the needles. Later, it gets darker and acquires brown markings **(2a)**. It then rests on the twigs. Most Europe: southern B. only.

95

1

1. Convolvulus Hawk *Agrius convolvuli*

This migrant resembles the privet hawk, but has no black patch on the thorax. Hind wings are grey. It has a fast, darting flight and hovers to feed at flowers. Its tongue is up to 13cm long. The larva may be bright green or purplish brown with darker spots. It eats bindweeds and morning glory. Summer visitor to most Europe: rare in B.

2. Elephant Hawk *Deilephila elpenor*

This attractive moth can be seen hovering at honeysuckle flowers at dusk in June. At rest, its wings are swept back like an arrowhead. The larva eats mainly willowherb in summer. When disturbed, it pulls its head into the thoracic region, which swells up to display the eye-spots (**2a**), and frightens birds by swaying to and fro. All Europe.

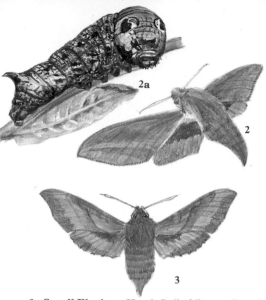

3. Small Elephant Hawk *Deilephila porcellus*

Slightly smaller and more colourful than **2**, this moth flies May/July. It feeds at rhododrendrons, honeysuckle, and other tubular flowers. Like **2**, it sweeps its wings back like an arrowhead when at rest. The larva resembles that of **2**, but has no horn. It feeds mainly on bedstraws, but also on willowherbs and purple loosestrife. Like most hawk-moth larvae, it feeds at night. Most Europe.

1. **Spurge Hawk** *Hyles euphorbiae*
This moth closely resembles **3**, but its front wings
are slightly broader and the hind wings have a
broad pink band. The amount of pink on front
wings varies a good deal. The moth flies June/July.
Its striking larva is black with red stripes and red
and cream blotches – superb warning coloration. It
feeds on various spurges in late summer. Most
Europe: a rare summer visitor to B.

1. Striped Hawk *Hyles lineata livornica*
This strongly migrant moth gets its name from the distinct white veins on front wing. It flies May/June and again in late summer, visiting nectar-rich flowers like honeysuckle, petunias, and red valerian. The larva is dark green or black with a yellowish spots. It feeds June/July, food plants including bedstraws, docks, and the grape vine. A summer visitor to Europe from Africa: rare in B.

3. Bedstraw Hawk *Hyles galii*
This moth flies May/July, mainly in sandy regions. It is most common in coastal areas. Closely related to **1**, it can be distinguished by the unbroken brown band on front edge of wing. The larva ranges from dark green to black, with large pale spots on the back. It feeds on bedstraws in summer. Most Europe: sporadic summer visitor to B.

1. *Hyles vespertilio*

Uniform greyish wings distinguish this from other hawk-moths. It flies June-July in mountainous areas, with a partial second brood August/September in some of the valleys. The larva is greyish brown with a row of pale spots on each side. It has no horn. It feeds on willowherb, especially the fine-leaved *Epilobium rosmarinifolium*, in summer. S. & C. Europe: not B.

2

2. *Hyles hippophaes*
This moth flies June/July, normally in coastal areas and in river valleys where its food plant, sea buckthorn, grows on the sands and gravels. It readily comes to light. The larva is pale greyish green with an orange spot near the tail horn. It blends well with the foliage and fruit of the food plant. S. & C. Europe: not B.

3. *Proserpinus proserpina*
This small hawk-moth usually has clear green front wings with a darker band, but there are also greyish and brown forms. It flies in summer. The larva is dull green at first, becoming greyish brown with a broad buff band on each side. The horn is small in the early stages and disappears altogether when the larva becomes brown. It feeds on willowherbs and evening primrose, and also on purple loosestrife. S. & C. Europe: not B.

1. Narrow-bordered Bee Hawk *Hemaris tityus*
This day-flying moth looks remarkably like a large
bee, but it has a much faster flight than the bumble
bees. It darts from flower to flower, hovering in
front of each to feed. It flies May/June, and again in
August in S. Europe. The wings are clothed with
loose scales at first, but these drop off during the first
flight, leaving just the edges and the veins brown.
The larva, green with rows of purple dots, feeds on
scabious. All Europe.

2

2. Humming-bird Hawk
Macroglossum stellatarum
This day-flying moth gets its name from its habit of hovering in front of flowers like a humming-bird. Front wings are brown and hind wings deep orange. It flies throughout summer, with three or even four broods in S. Europe, where adults hibernate in caves and buildings. Spring migration takes many moths north and a new generation flies late summer. Some adults may hibernate in southern B. The larva is either green or brown with white dots and a bluish horn. It feeds mainly on bedstraws. All Europe.

3. Broad-bordered Bee Hawk
Hemaris fuciformis
The broader wing borders distinguish this species from **1**. It flies May/June in sunshine and is most often found in woodland glades and around the edges of woodlands. A second brood flies in August in S. Europe. The larva is bright green on top and reddish brown underneath. it feeds on honeysuckle and bedstraw. All Europe: southern B. only.

Oak Hawk *Marumba quercus*
This large moth, coloured quite unlike any other
European hawk-moth, flies June/August, usually in
hilly districts. The larva ranges from yellow to bluish
green and has a blue horn. There are seven oblique
yellow stripes on each side. It can be found July/
August, feeding on the evergreen leaves of the cork
oak, but it is very well camouflaged. It will also eat
other oak leaves. S. Europe.

Death's-head Hawk *Acherontia atropos*
This famous species gets its name from the skull-like
pattern on the thorax. Hind wings are yellow with
black bands. A resident of Africa, it migrates to
Europe each spring. The larva, up to 13cm long, is
green or yellow with white and bluish diagonal
stripes. It feeds mainly on potato and nightshades.
Summer visitor to most Europe: rare in B.

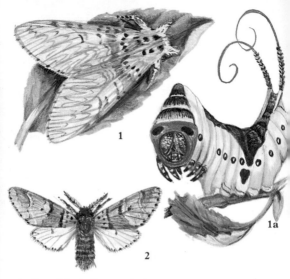

1. Puss Moth *Cerura vinula*
This furry moth flies May/July. The larva **(1a)** pulls in its head when disturbed and extrudes its 'tails', which are modified claspers. It eats willow and poplar July/August. All Europe.

2. Poplar Kitten *Furcula bifida*
Flying May/July, this moth is closely related to **1** and has a similar larva feeding on poplars July/September. Most Europe: southern B. only.

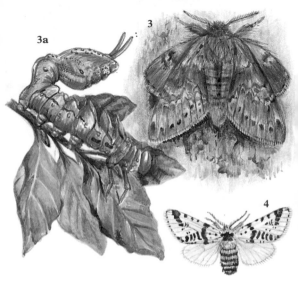

3. Lobster Moth *Stauropus fagi*

Named for its unusual larva **(3a)**, this moth flies
May/July. At rest, it resembles a bunch of dead
leaves. The larva eats oak, beech, birch, and hazel
July/September. Most Europe: southern B. only.

4. *Neoharpyia verbasci*

This moth flies April/May and again in late summer.
Its larva, like that of **1** but smaller, feeds on sallow in
June and in Autumn. Spain and S. France.

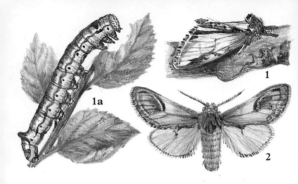

1. Lesser Swallow Prominent *Pheosia gnoma*

On the wing May/June and again in August, this moth is very well camouflaged when at rest on twigs and bark. The hind wings are off-white. It is very similar to the swallow prominent (*P. tremula*), but the latter lacks the distinct white wedge-shaped mark at the back of the front wing. The larva **(1a)** feeds on birch June/October. Most Europe.

2. Pebble Prominent *Eligmodonta ziczac*

Named for the pebble-like blotch near the wing-tip, this moth flies May/October, with a single brood in the north and two or three elsewhere (two in southern B.). The larva is greyish-pink with two large humps on the back and it feeds mainly on willows. Like most prominent larvae, it rests with both front and hind end of the body raised, holding on with just four pairs of prolegs. Most Europe.

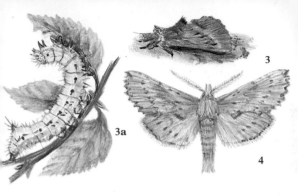

3. Coxcomb Prominent *Ptilodon capucina*

At rest, this moth clearly displays the little tufts of scales on the hind edge of front wing, which are so characteristic of the prominents and which give the group its name. They stand up about halfway along the back. This species flies May/June and August/September in wooded regions. The larva (**3a**) feeds on various trees June/October. Most Europe.

4. Pale Prominent *Pterostoma palpina*

This moth has very long palps sticking forward from the head. It flies in May, and again in late summer in the south. At rest, the wings are held tightly to the sides of the body to resemble a broken twig. The larva is bluish-green with a yellow stripe on each side. It feeds on poplars and willows June/July and again in autumn. Most Europe.

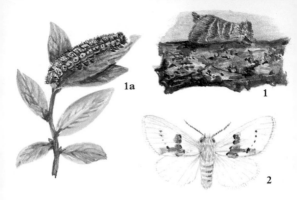

1. **Small Chocolate-tip** *Clostera pigra*

This small moth flies in damp woods and fens May/
June and, except in the north, again July/September.
At rest, with the tip of the abdomen raised, it resembles
a broken twig. The larva **(1a)** feeds on willows May/
July and again in autumn, usually in a 'tent' of leaves
fixed together with silk. Most Europe, but not far
south. (Chocolate-tip (*C. curtula*) is larger, with more
prominent chocolate wing-tips.)

2. **White Prominent** *Leucodonta bicoloria*

This moth flies in birch woods and scrub in June and
sometimes takes to the wing in the daytime. The
larva is pale green, with yellow and dark green lines,
and it feeds on birch June/August. Most Europe:
believed extinct in B.

3. **Buff-tip** *Phalera bucephala*

This very common moth flies May/July. At rest, the
wings are rolled tightly round the body and the buff
wing-tips, together with the brown hairs of the thorax,
give it the appearance of a broken twig. The larvae
are deep yellow with black stripes and spots and
gregarious when young. They feed July/October on
a wide variety of deciduous trees, often becoming
orchard pests. Most Europe.

4. **Figure-of-Eight** *Diloba caeruleocephala*

The clear figure 8 (sometimes 88) on front wing
gives this moth its name. It flies in late autumn and
often comes to lighted windows. The larva is bluish-
grey with yellow stripes and it feeds on hawthorn
and other rosaceous trees May/July. Most Europe:
rare in Scotland.

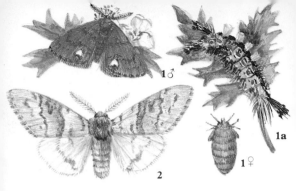

1. **Vapourer** *Orgyia antiqua*
The male of this species flies in the daytime from June onwards, with up to three broods. It flies rapidly along hedgerows in search of the wingless female. The latter never moves away from her cocoon and lays her eggs on it after mating. The larva (**1a**) feeds from spring onwards on a variety of deciduous trees. Most Europe.

2. **Pale Tussock** *Dasychira pudibunda*
This moth flies May/July. Female is larger and paler, although the depth of colour is variable. The larva is green or yellow with four dense tufts or brushes of white hair on the upper side. There is also a more slender, reddish tuft towards the back. It feeds throughout the summer on oak, birch, and many other deciduous trees. N. & C. Europe: southern B. only.

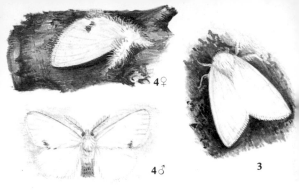

3. White Satin *Leucoma salicis*
This moth is most common in coastal areas, although it is not confined to them. It flies June/August. The larva is hairy, essentially red and black with large white patches on top. It feeds on willows and poplars, hibernating when small and completing its growth in spring. Most Europe.

4. Yellow-tail *Euproctis similis*
Also known as the gold-tail, this moth is named for the tuft of golden hair at the back. The tuft is much larger in female, who uses the hair to cover her eggs. She is larger than male altogether. The black dots may be absent from the wings. It flies June/August in all kinds of habitats. The hairy larva is black with white spots and a red dorsal stripe. It feeds on various trees in autumn and again after hibernation. Most Europe.

1 ♀

1 ♂

1. Gypsy Moth *Lymantria dispar*

Males fly by day July/September, often in large swarms. Females do not fly. Eggs are laid close to the cocoon, often on bark or in rock crevices, and covered with hairs from the female's body. The young larvae are very hairy and are blown about by the wind. Older ones are greenish-grey with bluish and reddish warts. They feed April/June on many kinds of deciduous trees and are serious forest pests in many places. Most Europe: extinct in B.

2. Oak Processionary Moth
Thaumetopoea processionea
It is the larva (**2a**) that gives this species its name. It lives communally in silken tents on oak trunks and branches May/June and goes out in processions to feed on the leaves at night. The leaders march in single file, but the others walk several abreast, making a V-shaped column. Adults fly August/ September. S. & C. Europe: not B. (Pine processionary larvae live in nests among pine needles and march in single file. They hibernate in the nests and pupate in spring.)

3. Black Arches *Lymantria monacha*
Flying July/August, the male often visits lights, but female is larger and less active. The larva is dark grey with tufts of paler hairs. It feeds on oaks and conifers April/June, sometimes being a serious plantation pest. Most Europe: southern B. only.

1. Peach Blossom *Thyatira batis*

This very pretty and easily recognised moth flies in wooded areas May/July and sometimes again in autumn. The depth of the pink colour varies, and the pink is sometimes replaced by a light orange. The larva **(1a)** habitually rests with the tail end up in the air. It feeds on bramble July/September. N. & C. Europe: mainly southern B.

2. Buff Arches *Habrosyne pyritioides*

This moth flies June/July, and occasionally again in autumn, and is common in gardens, hedgerows, and wooded areas in general. It commonly comes to light. It rests with its wings held steeply roof-wise over the body, and is then well concealed among dead leaves on the ground. The larva is rusty brown with a broad black line on the back. It feeds on bramble July/September. Most Europe: not Scotland.

3. *Syntomis phegea*

This day-flying moth inhabits sunny slopes June/ July. It resembles the burnets in its sluggish behaviour when feeding on flowers, and is quite easily picked up. Flight is straight, but slow, although the wings beat rapidly. The white spots vary in size and may join up. Female is more heavily built, with shorter wings, and flies much less than male. The larva is black with brown tufts and feeds on grasses and other low-growing plants in autumn and again after hibernation. S. & C. Europe: not B.

4. *Dysauxes punctata*

This species is related to **3** and flies in sunshine June/July. It favours warm, south-facing slopes with scattered trees and shrubs. The spot pattern varies. The larva is hairy and feeds on tree-trunk lichens in spring. S. & C. Europe: not B.

1. Four-spotted Footman *Lithosia quadra*

The female of this species is easily recognised by the two large spots on each front wing. Front wings of male are grey with a yellow base and a black streak on front edge. It flies in wooded areas July/September. The larva is hairy, like most footmen larvae, and feeds on lichens. Most Europe.

2. Rosy Footman *Miltochrista miniata*

This is a high-flying species found in wooded areas June/August. The amount of black on the wings varies a good deal. The hairy larva feeds on lichens August/May. Most Europe: southern B. only.

3. Common Footman *Eilema lurideola*

This is one of several similar species, but can be recognised because the yellow stripe on the front margin of wing tapers and does not reach the wing-tip. It flies in wooded areas June/August. At rest, the wings are wrapped loosely round the body. The larva feeds on lichens. Most Europe.

4. **Dew Moth** *Setina irrorella*
The wings of this moth are thinly scaled. Male is larger and paler than female. It flies June/August on cliffs and in other rocky places. The larva feeds on lichens in autumn and again in spring after hibernation. Most Europe in hilly regions: rare in B (mainly coastal).

5. **Red-necked Footman** *Atolmis rubricollis*
Easily identified by its red neck, this moth flies in woodland May/August. The hairy larva feeds on lichens July/October. S. & C. Europe: mainly southern B.

6. **Feathered Footman** *Spiris striata*
This moth flies May/July in rough, grassy places and especially on heathland. Female lacks the heavy black veins on the front wings and has plain antennae. The larvae feed on various herbaceous plants and hibernate gregariously in a silken web. Much of Europe and especially common in south: not B.

1. Crimson Speckled *Utetheisa pulchella*

This very attractive little moth flies in bright sunshine April/October. Hind wings are white with a black border. The larva is greyish with black and grey bristles and white lines. An orange bar crosses each segment. It feeds on forget-me-not, borage, and other herbaceous plants autumn/spring, with sporadic hibernation. S. & C. Europe (mainly Mediterranean): occasional visitor to B.

2. Ruby Tiger *Phragmatobia fuliginosa*

This fast-flying species is on the wing May/July. A partial 2nd brood flies in autumn. Northern specimens may be darker, with hind wings sooty black although still translucent. The larva (**2a**) is blackish with a red stripe and spots on the back and tufts of brownish hairs. It eats various low-growing plants in summer. Most Europe.

3. *Euprepia pudica*
The ground colour of the front wings of this tiger moth ranges from almost white to deep pink. It is extremely common late summer and autumn in Mediterranean areas. The larva is greyish-brown with short hairs and it feeds on grasses autumn/April, often being quite active on mild winter days. S. Europe.

4. Wood Tiger *Parasemia plantaginis*
Despite its name, this moth is more common on heathland and open grassland than in woods, although it does inhabit lightly wooded areas. It flies June/August, the male flying in sunshine. Female flies at night and also on sunny afternoons. The larva is blackish, with tufts of black, reddish, and grey hairs. It feeds on a variety of low-growing plants in autumn and again after hibernation. N. & C. Europe: mostly northern & western B.

1. White Ermine *Spilosoma lubricipeda*
This very common moth flies May/July and sometimes again in autumn in gardens and many other habitats. It regularly come to lights. The spots on front wing vary in number and density and are sometimes almost absent. Occasionally, they join up to form streaks. Hind wings have just a few black spots. The abdomen is yellow. The larva **(1a)** is dark and furry, with a red line along the back. It feeds on a wide variety of low-growing plants July/September and walks very quickly. Most Europe.

2. Buff Ermine *Spilosoma lutea*
Closely related to **1**, this species has very similar habits and flies at the same time. Female is paler and the number and arrangement of the black markings vary. The larva resembles that of **1**, but is paler and has no red line. Most Europe.

3. **Muslin Moth** *Diaphora mendica*

The wings of this species are thinly scaled, and quite translucent in female, thus giving the moth its name. Female resembles **1**, but her translucence and white abdomen distinguish her. She flies May/June, mainly by day, but male flies by night. The larva is like that of **2**, but the hairs are much paler. It feeds on various low-growing plants June/September. N. & C. Europe.

4. **Clouded Buff** *Diacrisia sannio*

Female is smaller and has deep orange wings: hind wing has black patch near base. It flies over moorland and heathland May/September, male being active in sunshine and female at night. There are two broods in most parts of Europe, but only one (June/July) in B. The larva is brown and hairy with a broad white stripe on the back. It eats various low-growing plants before and after hibernation. Most Europe.

1

1. Garden Tiger *Arctia caja*

The bold, bright colours of the various species of tiger moths warn birds that the moths have unpleasant tastes and irritating hairs. The garden tiger flies June/August and commonly comes to lighted windows. But despite its bright colours, it is rarely seen by day, for it hides among the vegetation. The markings are very variable. The larva is the well-known 'woolly bear' – a very hairy, dark brown creature. It begins feeding in summer, but hibernates when small and completes its growth in spring, when it is common on low-growing plants in gardens and hedgerows. All Europe.

2. Cream-spot Tiger *Arctia villica*

Another variable species, this moth flies May/July. Its larva resembles that of **1**, but has bright red legs and a red head (all black in *A. caja*), and its life history is also similar. S. & C. Europe: southern B. only (mainly coastal).

3. *Pericallia matronula*

This large moth flies May/June, often taking to the wing in the daytime. The spots vary in size and may be larger than shown here on front wing. Hind wing spots may be separate, or joined to form a band as seen here. The larva is dark brown or black, with long reddish-brown hairs, and takes two years to mature – hibernating through two winters. It feeds on a wide range of plants, including willow and dandelion. Much of Europe, from eastern France eastwards.

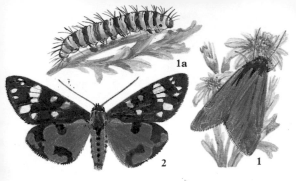

1. **Cinnabar** *Tyria jacobaeae*

The dull black front wings, marked with brilliant red (cinnabar) readily identify this species. Hind wings are red with black margins. It flies May/July in rough grassy places, often taking wing when disturbed in the daytime. Flight is rather weak. The larva **(1a)** is a very familiar object, feeding communally on ragwort July/August and displaying some very effective warning coloration. Most Europe: mainly coastal in northern B.

2. **Scarlet Tiger** *Callimorpha dominula*

Flying by day, this moth inhabits fens and other damp places June/July. The spot pattern varies and the red is sometimes replaced by yellow. Hind wings are occasionally black. The larva is black and hairy with red and yellow spots. It feeds on many shrubs and herbaceous plants in autumn and again after hibernation. Most Europe: southern B. only.

3. Jersey Tiger *Euplagia quadripunctaria*

This moth flies by night and by day July/September, and in parts of S. Europe it roosts communally in dull weather. The larva is dark and hairy with a yellowish stripe on the back and white spots on the sides. It hibernates when small and feeds up on many low-growing plants in spring. S. & C. Europe: common in Channel Islands, but only south-western coasts in B. (introduced in 19th century).

4. Short-cloaked Moth *Nola cucullatella*

At rest, the wings are swept back to form an arrow-head shape and the dark patch at base of each front wing looks like a short cloak around the 'shoulders'. It flies June/July. The larva is reddish-brown with grey hairs and whitish spots. It hibernates when young and completes its growth on blackthorn and other rosaceous trees and shrubs in spring. Much of Europe, but local: not Scotland.

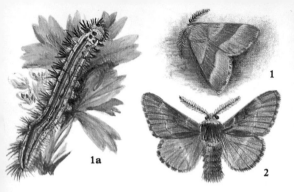

1. Lackey *Malacosoma neustria*

This very common, fast-flying moth is on the wing July/August. Female is larger, with relatively longer wings. The colour ranges from pale buff to deep reddish brown. The eggs are laid on twigs and they hatch in spring. The brightly coloured larvae **(1a)** live communally in silken webs on a variety of deciduous trees and are often orchard pests. They become solitary shortly before pupating. Most Europe: southern B. only.

2. December Moth *Poecilocampa populi*

Named for its October/December flight period, this thinly-scaled moth varies from dark grey to sooty brown. Females are larger, with longer wings. It flies mainly in wooded areas, but males often come to lighted windows. The dark brown, hairy larva feeds on various trees April/June. N. & C. Europe.

3. Small Eggar *Eriogaster lanestris*

The wings of this moth are quite thinly scaled. Male is smaller and resembles **2** in shape, but is browner and has white marks like female. It flies February/March. The larvae feed on hawthorn and blackthorn April/July and spend most of their lives in silken webs. Each is black with reddish brown blotches edged with pale yellow. N. & C. Europe.

4. Oak Eggar *Lasiocampa quercus*

The male flies rapidly by day May/August, but female is slower and flies by night to scatter her eggs. She is larger than male and yellowish-brown all over. Northern moths are usually darker than southern ones. The hairy brown larva feeds on bramble, heather, and various other trees and shrubs. It hibernates when small and completes its growth in spring and summer. Most Europe.

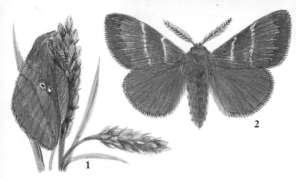

1. The Drinker *Philudoria potatoria*

This heavily-built moth gets its name from the dew-drinking habits of its larva. The adult female is a little larger than male and much paler, being yellowish-brown. The moth flies June/August in many grassy habitats and is often common on roadside verges. The hairy brown larva feeds on coarse grasses in autumn and again in spring after hibernation. It forms a long papery cocoon on grass stems. Most Europe.

2. Fox Moth *Macrothylacia rubi*

The female of this species is much greyer and has longer wings. It flies May/July on moorland and heathland and in open woodland. Males are active by day and the females lay their eggs at night. The velvety brown larva feeds mainly on bramble and heather in late summer. It hibernates when fully grown and pupates in spring. Most Europe.

3a

3

3. The Lappet *Gastropacha quercifolia*

Flying June/July, this moth is usually purplish-brown, but may be yellowish-brown in S. Europe. Female is up to twice the size of male. At rest on vegetation or the ground, the hind wings are spread out more or less flat, and front wings are held roof-wise over the body, giving the moth the appearance of a bunch of dead leaves. The furry larva **(3a)** feeds on blackthorn and other related trees and also on sallow. Young larvae sit tightly against the twigs and are very hard to see. They hibernate when partly grown and complete their growth in spring. S. & C. Europe: southern B. only.

1. Kentish Glory *Endromis versicolora*
Female is much larger and paler, with greyish-brown
front wings and almost white hind wings. Hind wings
of male are deep orange. The moth is on the wing
March/ May on moorland and in open woodland.
Males fly very strongly in the sunshine. Females fly
at night. The larva **(1a)** feeds on birch May/July and
can be mistaken for a hawk-moth caterpillar because
of the horn-like growth at the hind end, although
this is much stouter than a hawk-moth's horn. N. &
C. Europe: recent British specimens all from Scotland.

2

3

2. *Lemonia dumi*

This moth flies late autumn in woodland clearings, especially in the native pine forests of the north and the mountains. Males fly by day and are fast and erratic. Female is lighter in colour and flies at night. The larva is dark brown, with yellowish-brown hairs, and feeds May/August on dandelions and other low-growing plants. N. & C. Europe: not B.

3. *Odonestis pruni*

Flying in lightly wooded areas June/August, this moth closely resembles the related drinker moth (p.130), but differs in having just one white spot on front wing. Female is larger and has much redder wings than male. The larva is hairy, bluish-grey on the back and orange-red below. It feeds on blackthorn and many other trees in autumn and again in spring after hibernation. S. & C. Europe: not B.

1. Giant Peacock Moth *Saturnia pyri*

With wings spanning up to 15cm, this is the largest of the European moths. It flies in May and, unlike the closely related emperor **(2)**, both sexes fly by night. They are often mistaken for bats. Hind wings also bear eye-spots. The mature larva is yellowish-green, with rings of pale blue warts and long, clubbed spines. In its early stages it is black with rings of red or orange round it. It feeds on blackthorn, ash, and various other trees, including orchard species, in summer. S. Europe, occasionally as far north as Paris.

2. **Emperor Moth** *Saturnia pavonia*

This smaller relative of **1** flies April/May on heathland and along hedgerows and woodland margins. Male flies rapidly by day in search of the larger and much greyer female. He can pick up her scent from as much as 2km away. She flies and lays her eggs at night. The larva (**2a**) feeds on heather, blackthorn, bramble, and other shrubs May/July. In its early stages it is black and orange. Most Europe.

Tau Emperor *Aglia tau*

The ground colour of the male of this striking moth is usually tawny yellow, but it may also be very deep brown. Female is larger and paler. The eye-spots vary in size. Underside has eye-spots only on front wing, hind wing bearing a star-like or arrow-like white mark. The insect is on the wing April/May, the male flying by day in search of female. The latter is active mainly at night, but does not fly much. The larva is pale green, with red spines on each end until the final moult. It feeds on birch and other trees June/July and looks very much like a rolled-up leaf. Much of Europe: not B.

Spanish Moon Moth *Graellsia isabellae*
Perhaps Europe's most beautiful moth, this species
is related to the Atlas moth and some of the other
large silk moths. Female has shorter tails than male.
It flies spring and early summer. The larva is bright
green with a reddish-brown stripe on the back. It
feeds on maritime pine and some other conifers in
summer. Once confined to the Iberian Peninsula,
the species now also lives in the French Alps, where
it was probably introduced.

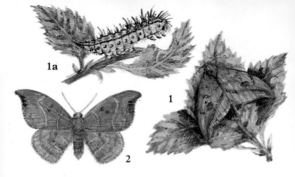

1. Pebble Hook-tip *Drepana falcataria*

Like all hook-tips, this moth has a curved point or
hook on front wing-tip. The dark mark in the centre
of front wing is the 'pebble'. The ground colour
ranges from dirty white to deep brown. It flies May/
September, with two broods. The larva **(1a)** feeds
on birch June/October. Like other hook-tip larvae,
it has no claspers and the body tapers to a point.
N. & C. Europe.

2. Oak Hook-tip *Drepana binaria*

This moth flies May/June and again in August in
lightly wooded areas. Female is larger and paler,
especially in hind wing. Male, in common with other
hook-tips, has slightly feathery antennae. The larva
is basically brown, with a two-pronged hump on 3rd
segment. It feeds on oak and birch and, like other
hook-tip larvae, it rests with both ends raised from
surface. S. & C. Europe.

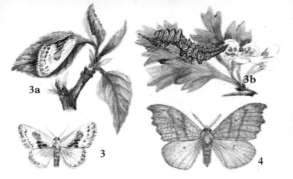

3. Chinese Character *Cilix glaucata*

The variable silvery lines within the dark blotches probably gave this moth its name. At rest (**3a**), it looks extremely like a bird dropping. It flies April/September, with two broods, inhabiting hedgerows, gardens, and woodland margins. It commonly comes to light. Although the adult has no hooked wing-tips, the larva (**3b**) is typical of the hook-tip family. It feeds June/October on hawthorn and blackthorn. Most Europe.

4. Scalloped Hook-tip *Drepana lacertinaria*

The ragged edges of the wings make this an easily identifiable species. It flies May/June and again in August in woodlands and on heathlands. The wings are folded round the body at rest and the insect then resembles a shrivelled leaf. The larva is reddish-brown with two double-pronged humps near the front. It eats birch June/September. Most Europe.

1. **Orange Underwing** *Archiearis parthenias*

This moth is on the wing on sunny days in March and April, mainly in birch woods. The male flies quite fast and usually high up in the trees, but female is less active and spends much of her time sitting on the birch twigs. The orange of hind wing is sometimes replaced by yellow. The larva **(1a)** feeds on the catkins and leaves of birch April/June. Most Europe.

2. **Chimney Sweeper** *Odezia atrata*

This well-named little moth is sooty black when freshly emerged, but becomes dark brown after a few days on the wing. There is a narrow white fringe to the front wing-tip. It flies in the sunshine June/July, inhabiting roadside verges and other grassy places. The wings are held flat at rest and swept back into a triangle. The larva, pale green with darker lines and red spiracles, eats pignut flowers in spring. Most Europe.

3. *Euchrostes indigenata*

Sitting with wings outstretched, this little moth blends beautifully with the leaves. Its bright green colour is found in very few other moths. It flies throughout summer and autumn, with two or three broods. The larva is bright green, tinged with red at each end, and it feeds on spurges in summer and autumn. S. Europe.

4. **Purple-bordered Gold** *Sterrha muricata*

This pretty little moth ranges from almost entirely yellow to almost completely purple, but front margin is always purple. Purple forms are more common in the north. It flies June/July in fens and other damp habitats and is most often on the wing at around sunrise. The larva is pale brown, marked with irregular black lines. It eats marsh cinquefoil, plantains, and some other herbaceous plants. Most Europe.

1. Large Emerald *Geometra papilionaria*

This beautiful moth flies June/July in wooded areas. As in all emeralds, the full colour lasts for only a few days and older specimens are much paler. The white cross-lines may be very faint, or even absent. The twig-like larva feeds on birch, hazel, and beech in late summer. When the leaves fall, it goes to sleep on a twig. It wakes in spring and continues to feed, becoming greener as the new leaves unfold. Most Europe.

2. Essex Emerald *Thetidia smaragdaria*

The wings vary from yellowish to bluish-green and typically have two white cross-lines on front wing, although one or both lines may be missing. It flies June/July. The grey larva feeds on sea wormwood in autumn and again after hibernation. It covers itself with fragments of food plant. Much of Europe: v. rare in B. (coastal Essex only).

3. Grass Emerald *Pseudoterpna pruinata*
The blue-green of the freshly emerged moth fades to a bluish-grey after a few days and it is then hard to recognise it as an emerald. The cross-lines are often indistinct. It flies June/August over moorland and damp grassland. The larva, green with darker green and white lines, feeds on broom and gorse in late summer and again after hibernation. N. & C. Europe.

4. Blotched Emerald *Comibaena pustulata*
The pale markings vary to some extent, but the wing pattern easily distinguishes this species from the other emeralds. It flies in and around oak woods June/August. The larva is reddish-brown and covers itself with particles of leaves and bud scales, held on by silken strands. It feeds on oak in autumn and again in spring after hibernation. N. & C. Europe: southern B. only.

1. Blood-vein *Calothysanis amata*

The 'blood vein' stripe across all four wings ranges
from pink to purple. It flies along damp hedgerows
and woodland margins, and also on waste ground
May/July, with a partial 2nd brood in August. The
larva is greyish, with four dark spots on the back, and
it feeds on docks and other low-growing plants from
late summer to spring. Most Europe.

2. *Idaea ostrinaria*

This pretty moth flies in June. Its ground colour
ranges from pale to deep yellow and the purple tones
also vary. The purple is much more extensive in
some Spanish specimens. The reddish-brown larva
is short and wrinkled and clothed with fine hairs
which trap pollen as a camouflage. It feeds on pollen
at first, and then the stamens, petals, and leaves of
low-growing plants. Mediterranean area.

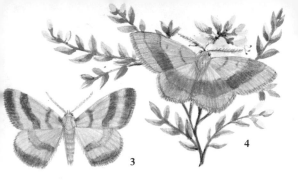

3. *Rhodostrophia calabra*

This beautiful moth has a variable yellow ground colour. The rosy margins and central band on all wings are redder in the more southerly areas. Flight is weak and unsustained April/July. The larva feeds on broom and related plants, hibernating when small and completing growth in spring. It is yellowish-brown or grey with short black bristles. S. Europe and warm valleys in central areas: not B.

4. *Rhodostrophia vibicaria*

This species resembles **3**, but the ground colour is paler and the pink bands have sharper edges. Hind wing is also strongly angled. It flies April/August with two broods in most places but a single brood (June/July) in northern parts of range. The larva varies from yellow to brown and feeds on broom and related plants. S. & C. Europe: not B.

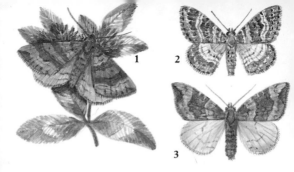

1. Shaded Broad-bar *Ortholitha chenopodiata*
This species resembles a small mallow moth (p.148) but lacks the scalloped effect on wing margins. Hind wings may be much browner than shown here. It flies July/August. The larva feeds September/June on grasses and leguminous plants. Most Europe.

2. Common Carpet *Epirrhöe alternata*
The dark markings on this very common moth may be black or brownish, and the dark bands may be so wide that the pale areas of front wings are almost obscured. It flies May/June and August/September. The larva feeds on bedstraws. Most Europe.

3. Northern Spinach *Lygris populata*
Front wings may be almost pure yellow with fine cross lines, or completely brown. Northern specimens may be almost black. It flies July/August, mainly in upland woods and moorland. The larva feeds on bilberry and other shrubs. N. & C. Europe.

4. Lace Border *Scopula ornata*
This dainty moth flies May/June and August/
September over areas of rough grassland, especially
on chalk and limestone soils. The larva is long and
slender, light brown above and greyish below, with
several dark V-shaped marks on the back. It feeds on
wild thyme and marjoram July/August and October/
May. S. & C. Europe: southern B. only.

5. Clay Triple-lines *Cosymbia linearia*
The wings of this moth vary from pale yellow to light
brick-coloured. The inner and outer cross-lines are
often missing. It flies May/June and August/Sep-
tember, rarely moving far from beech woods. The
larva is pale brown with some yellowish streaks and
lines. It feeds on beech leaves June/July and again in
September. S. & C. Europe: southern B. only.

1. The Mallow *Larentia clavaria*
The front wings of this species range from pale brown to chocolate, the cross bands often being indistinct. The chequered margins give a distinctly scalloped appearance to the wings. It flies September/November and spends the daytime hiding among low-growing vegetation. When disturbed, it flies surprisingly quickly for such a flimsy insect. The larva hatches in early spring and feeds on mallows and hollyhocks. It is slender and green with faint darker lines on the back. Much of Europe.

2. The Vestal *Rhodometra sacraria*
The front wings of this moth range from pale yellow to orange-brown, and the stripe may be crimson, brown, or blackish. It flies for much of the summer. The larva is long and green, with reddish and olive-green lines. It eats docks and other low-growing plants. S. & C. Europe: rare visitor to B.

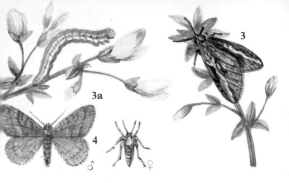

3. The Streak *Chesias legatella*

This well-named moth flies September/October and can be found sitting on broom twigs by day. Male has fawn streaks and markings, whereas the streak of female is very pale. The larva (3a) feeds on broom leaves in spring. Most Europe.

4. Winter Moth *Operophtera brumata*

This moth flies throughout the winter, from October to February. Males often come to lighted windows on cold, damp nights and sit there for hours. The wings are swept back to form a more or less triangular outline. Female is wingless and sits on tree trunks after emerging from her pupa in the soil. After mating, she lays her eggs on the bare twigs. The larva is pale green, with a darker stripe along the back and white lines on the sides. It feeds April/May on various trees and bushes, often becoming a pest in apple orchards. Most Europe.

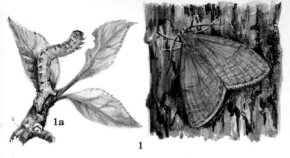

1a

1

1. November Moth *Oporinia dilutata*

The front wings of this species range from pale grey to sooty black, the cross lines being difficult to see in darker specimens. Hind wings are always pale grey. The moth is common in November, but actually flies September/January, often coming to lighted windows. The larva (**1a**) feeds on a wide variety of trees April/June. Most Europe.

2. Small Waved Umber *Horisme vitalbata*

When resting on tree trunks, this moth sits with its body horizontal and its wings spread well out to the sides. The prominent wing stripes thus run vertically and blend beautifully with the bark fissures. It flies April/September, with two broods, and is common in many gardens and hedgerows. The larva feeds on traveller's-joy June/October. It is greyish-brown, with three dark lines on the back. The central one forms a black spot in centre of each segment. S. & C. Europe: southern B. only.

3. Mottled Umber *Erannis defoliaria*

This very common species flies October/February in a wide range of habitats. Front wings of male are always speckly, but ground colour ranges from almost white to purplish-brown, the cross bands often being indistinct in darker specimens. At rest, the wings are swept back to form a triangular shape. Female is wingless and sits on bark and twigs. The larva is yellowish with brown patches and feeds April/May on various trees, often stripping whole branches. Most Europe.

1. Scallop Shell *Rheumaptera undulata*

This delicate moth flies June/July in moist woods. The brown and white chequer-board pattern around the edges gives all the wings a distinctly scalloped appearance. The larva is plump and reddish-brown, with pale lines running along it. It feeds on sallow, aspen, and bilberry August/October. Most Europe: mainly southern B.

2. The Spinach *Lygris mellinata*

This moth is very common in gardens, where it flies June/August. The wings vary in the amount of brown, and the ground colour ranges from pale buff to yellow. At rest, the front wings are held well out to the sides and hind wings are brought forward underneath them. The moth thus appears to have only one pair of wings and is easily mistaken for a dead leaf. The larva is pale green, with darker green and white lines, and it feeds on current bushes May/June. Most Europe: rarer in north.

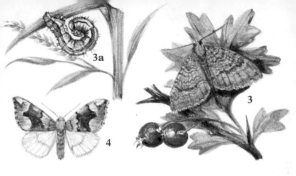

3. Yellow Shell

Camptogramma bilineata

This very common moth is shown here in its characteristic resting attitude, although it normally rests underneath the leaves. It lives in hedgerows, fields, and gardens all summer. The ground colour varies from bright yellow to brown and the cross bands may be almost black and somewhat wider than shown here. The larva (**3a**) ranges from green to reddish brown and feeds on grasses and many other low-growing plants August/May. Most Europe.

4. Barred Yellow *Cidaria fulvata*

This pretty moth flies June/July in gardens, woods, and hedgerows. At rest under the leaves the wings are swept back to form a triangular outline and the abdomen is often raised. The larva is green and wrinkled, with paler markings, and it feeds on wild roses May/June. Most Europe.

1. Garden Carpet *Xanthorhoe fluctuata*

The carpet moths nearly all have blotched or mottled wings – black and white in many species – resembling traditional carpet patterns. At rest, the wings are almost always swept back to form a triangular outline, with hind wings completely concealed by front ones. The blotchy patterns break up the outline and help to hide the moths, especially when they are resting on tree trunks or lichen-covered rocks. The garden carpet has two or more broods and flies spring/autumn in gardens and many other habitats. The contrast between the black and grey areas is often less marked than shown here. The larva varies from green to grey and feeds on cruciferous plants, including cabbages and wallflowers, June/October. Most Europe.

2. Green Carpet *Colostygia pectinaria*

This species is marked with a beautiful deep green in life, but the colour soon fades to a yellowish green after death. The moth flies May/July or even later, inhabiting hedgerows, woods, and scrubby places. It generally takes to the wing at about dusk. The larva is greenish brown, with reddish v-shaped marks on most segments. It hibernates when small and feeds up on bedstraws in spring. Most Europe.

3. **Pretty Chalk Carpet** *Melanthia procellata*

This moth flies June/August along hedgerows and woodland margins, mainly on chalk and limestone. The larva, pale brown with darker lines, feeds on traveller's-joy August/September. S. & C. Europe.

4. **Netted Carpet** *Eustroma reticulata*

This moth flies July/August, mainly in damp, shady places. Its larva is greenish-yellow, tinged with pink, and it feeds September/October on the flowers and seed capsules of touch-me-not balsam. N. & C. Europe: local in B., mostly northern.

5. **Twin-spot Carpet** *Colostygia didymata*

This moth varies from pale grey (especially in female) to almost black, and the twin spots are often rather less distinct than shown here. It flies July/August. The larva is green, with pinkish sides, and it feeds April/June on the flowers of grasses and other low-growing plants. Most Europe.

1. **Lime-speck Pug** *Eupithecia centaureata*

The pugs are small, flimsy moths mostly with rather slender front wings. At rest, the wings are spread out to each side and pressed flat against the leaves or bark, with the front edges of front wings more or less at right angles to the body. The lime-speck pug flies all summer, with two broods. It is not unlike a bird dropping when at rest and is easily overlooked on leaves as well as on bark. The larva is green, with or without red markings, and it feeds on the flowers of scabious and various composites, such as ragwort and knapweed. Most Europe.

2. **Netted Pug** *Eupithecia venosata*

The ground colour of this little moth ranges from grey to mid-brown. It flies May/June. The larva is greyish-brown above and greenish below, with darker lines along the back. It feeds June/August in the seed capsules of campions. Most Europe.

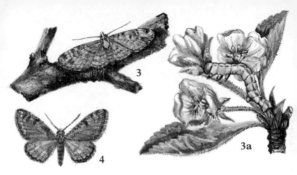

3. **Green Pug** *Chloroclystis rectangulata*
The green coloration is not always well developed in this species and the wings range from grey to black, making the moth very hard to find when resting on the tree trunks. It flies May/July. The larva **(3a)** is rather stouter than most pug moth larvae and feeds on the flowers of apples and pears April/May. Most Europe.

4. **Tawny-speckled Pug** *Eupithecia icterata*
The typical form of this species is shown here, but the fulvous patch is missing from many specimens and the wings are then dark brown all over. The moth flies June/August and enjoys feeding at flowers. It readily comes to light. The larva is reddish-brown with a white line through the spiracles and a row olive-brown spots on the back. It feeds on the flowers of yarrow and other composites July/October. Most Europe.

1. Magpie Moth *Abraxas grossulariata*
This weak-flying moth is very common in gardens
and hedgerows June/August. The ground colour
varies from white to yellow and the pattern is also
quite variable. The larva **(1a)** feeds on various trees
and shrubs, especially gooseberries and currants,
August/June. A black form **(1b)** occurs in some
places. The black and yellow pupa is enclosed in a
flimsy cocoon on the twigs. Most Europe.

2. Clouded Border *Lomaspilis marginata*
This delicate moth flies May/August, mainly in fairly moist wooded habitats. Male normally has a continuous dark band across the middle of front wing, and this continues across hind wing, but the pattern varies a good deal. There are two broods in most places. The larva is yellowish-green with three darker lines on the back. It feeds on willows and aspen June onwards. Most Europe.

3. Clouded Magpie *Abraxas sylvata*
Closely related to **1**, this moth flies May/July in woodland habitats, where it is most often found sitting on dog's mercury leaves and other, low-growing vegetation. Specimens with much greyer wings can be found in some places, and the black patches are reduced in some individuals. The larva is cream with black and yellow stripes and it feeds mainly on wych elm July/October. N. & C. Europe.

1. Light Emerald *Campaea margaritata*
Not closely related to the other emerald moths, this
species is delicate green when freshly emerged, but
soon fades to a dirty or brownish white. It flies
May/July, mainly in woods. The larva varies from
dark green to purplish brown and feeds September/
May on oak, birch, and various other trees. In the
winter, it often stirs to nibble buds and even the bark
of young twigs. Most Europe.

2. Large Thorn *Ennomos autumnaria*
This species flies August/October and is quite im-
pressive when it settles on a window pane, although
it lives more in woods than in gardens. Like many
other thorn moths, it often sits with its wings held up
above the body, although the wings are not normally
completely closed. The larva feeds on hawthorn and
various other trees and is extremely twig-like. Most
Europe: southern B. only.

3. **Scalloped Hazel** *Gonodontis bidentata*
The wings of this moth range from pale brown to almost black, but the most usual form is shown here. The area between the cross lines is often darker than the rest of the wings. It flies April/June. The twig-like larva is purplish, mottled with yellowish-brown, and it feeds on oak, birch, sallow, and many other trees July/October. Most Europe.

4. **Feathered Thorn** *Colotois pennaria*
The wings vary from very pale buff to a bright orange brick colour. Female often has a purplish tinge. The cross lines are sometimes quite close together. Male antennae are very feathery. It is mainly a woodland moth, flying October/November and regularly coming to lights. The larva is twig-like and feeds April/June on a wide variety of trees, especially oak, birch, and sallow. Most Europe.

1. Common White Wave *Deilinia pusaria*
This species flies May/August, mainly in wooded country, and has two broods. The inner cross bands may be missing and the wings are sometimes quite grey or even tinged with pink. The larva is purplish-brown with white spots and it feeds June/July and again in September on birch, sallow, and other trees. Most Europe. (The common wave (*D. exanthemata*) is similar, but its wings are speckled with grey and the two inner cross lines are much less regular.)

2. Clouded Silver *Bapta temerata*
Silky white wings with a greater or lesser amount of dark grey clouding make this an easily recognised species, although the clouding is sometimes almost absent in female. It flies May/June. The larva is green, with reddish spots in the final instar, and feeds July/August on Blackthorn, birch, and many other trees. Most Europe: mainly southern B.

3. Swallow-tailed Moth

Ourapteryx sambucaria

This attractive moth gets its name from the pointed 'tails' on hind wings. It flies June/July, its pale colours giving it a ghost-like appearance as it floats around the hedgerows. It is also common in gardens and along woodland margins. The larva (**3a**) is remarkably twig-like, even having bud-like 'warts' half-way along the body. It spends the daytime sitting rigid and motionless among the twigs. Ivy and hawthorn are its main foodplants. It feeds August/June, well protected during its winter sleep by its twig-like appearance. Most Europe.

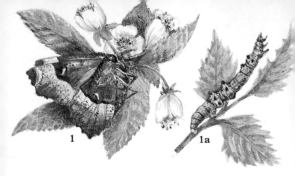

1. **Purple Thorn** *Selenia tetralunaria*

In common with the other thorn moths, this species regularly rests with wings held up above the body like those of a butterfly – either completely closed or forming a V. Underside and upperside are almost identical. It flies April/May and July/August. Summer moths are much paler than spring one seen here. The stick-like larva **(1a)** is a typical geometer, with only two pairs of prolegs including the claspers. It feeds on various trees in summer and autumn. S. & C. Europe: mainly southern B.

2. **Canary-shouldered Thorn**
Deuteronomos alniaria

Named for the canary-yellow thoracic hairs, which contrast with the darker yellow wings, this moth flies in wooded areas in autumn. The purplish-brown, twig-like larva feeds on birch, alder, and various other trees May/July. Most Europe.

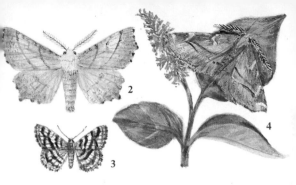

3. **Latticed Heath** *Chiasmia clathrata*

The ground colour of this flimsy moth ranges from white to yellowish-brown and the variable crosslines are dark brown or black. It flies mainly by day in grassy places April/May and again July/August. The larva, green with white lines, feeds on clover and trefoil June/September. Most Europe.

4. **Lilac Beauty** *Apeira syringaria*

This beautiful relative of **1** & **2** flies June/July and sometimes again in autumn. Female is slightly larger and paler than male. At rest, the wings are slightly raised and front ones are crinkled to resemble a dead leaf. The brownish larva carries two hook-like outgrowths halfway along the back. It feeds on honeysuckle, lilac, and privet, hibernating when small and completing growth May/June. Much of Europe: mainly southern B.

1. Scalloped Oak *Crocallis elinguaria*
The ground colour of this moth ranges from near-white, through primrose, to reddish-buff. The central band also varies in colour and intensity. It flies June/August and is a very common visitor to lighted windows. The larva is greyish with diamond-shaped marks on the back and it feeds on various trees and shrubs in spring. Most Europe.

2. Speckled Yellow *Pseudopanthera macularia*
Inhabiting lightly wooded areas, this pretty, day-flying moth flies May/June, usually only when the sun is shining. The brown markings vary in size, some heavily marked specimens appearing almost brown. Other moths are almost yellow. The larva is bright green and rather stout and feeds on wood sage and other labiates July/August. Most Europe.

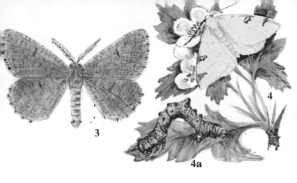

3. **Orange Moth** *Angerona prunaria*

Female is much paler than male and often quite yellow. Both sexes are occasionally brown, with the orange or yellow confined to a central band on each wing. It flies May/July in wooded regions. The brown, stick-like larva feeds on various trees, usually hibernating when small and completing growth in spring. Most Europe: mainly southern B.

4. **Brimstone Moth** *Opisthograptis luteolata*

Two generations of this pretty moth fly throughout the summer, but it is most common May/July. The larva **(4a)** is very twig-like and, like those of **1–3**, it is a typical looper, or geometer, with just two pairs of prolegs including the claspers. It feeds on hawthorn, blackthorn, and plum. Larvae from late summer eggs hibernate and complete their growth in spring. All Europe.

1. **Waved Umber** *Menophra abruptaria*

The resting moth holds its wings in such a way that the dark lines across all four wings come together to form a continuous stripe. This breaks up the outline of the moth and helps to blend it in with bark fissures. It flies April/June. The larva is greyish-brown with pinkish blotches on the back and it feeds mainly on privet and lilac May/August. Much of Europe: mainly southern B.

2. **Belted Beauty** *Lycia zonaria*

The ground colour of male ranges from white to greyish and the stripes from greyish-brown to black. It flies March/May, mainly in coastal areas. Female is wingless. The larva is green with darker freckles and a yellow stripe on the side. It feeds on a wide range of plants May/August. N. & C. Europe: mainly northern B.

3

4

3. **Oak Beauty** *Biston strataria*

This handsome moth flies February/May. Female
has slightly darker markings. At rest, the moth is
well camouflaged on tree trunks. The larva is purplish-
brown and very twig-like. Like the larva of the other
moths on this page, it is a geometer, with just two
pairs of prolegs including the claspers. It feeds on
oak, birch, and various other trees April/July. Most
Europe.

4. **Brindled Beauty** *Lycia hirtaria*

The wings of this species range from greyish to rich
brown and are often liberally speckled with yellow.
Female wings are longer and narrower. It flies March/
April and is often abundant in built-up areas. The
larva is reddish-brown and very stick-like and feeds
May/July on lime, elm, willow, and various fruit
trees. Most Europe.

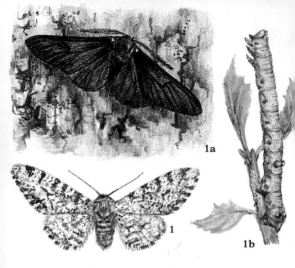

1a

1

1b

1. Peppered Moth *Biston betularia*

There are two main forms of this moth – the normal, speckled one and the black, melanic one **(1a)**. The melanic form was discovered in northern England in 1859 and gradually became more common as the industrial revolution blackened walls and tree trunks with soot. The black moth had an advantage over the normal form because it was well camouflaged. It escaped the attentions of birds and was able to breed. The normal form, very conspicuous on dark surfaces,

2

3

almost disappeared from many industrial areas. Today, as a result of pollution control, it is becoming commoner again. It has always been common in rural areas, and the melanic form also occurs in such areas today. It flies May/August. The larva **(1b)** has a deeply notched head and feeds July/September on a wide range of trees and shrubs. Most Europe.

2. *Gnophos variegata*

This moth flies in summer and its wings may have more blue-grey suffusion than shown here. The larva, yellowish-grey with prominent wrinkles and tubercles, feeds on wall rue fern in autumn and again after hibernation. S. & C. Europe: not B.

3. *Psodos quadrifaria*

This easily recognised moth flies by day June/July. In some specimens the yellow bands may be narrower. The larva is brown and feeds on various low-growing plants. Mountains of S. & C. Europe: not B.

1. Bordered White *Bupalus piniaria*
The light areas of male are white in northern Europe, including northern B, and yellow elsewhere. Females are orange-brown in the north and pale orange further south, always with brown wing-tips. Also known as the pine looper, the moth flies May/August. The larva, a typical looper, is long and green and marked with light and dark lines. It often causes serious damage to pines and other conifers. N. & C. Europe.

2. The Engrailed *Ectropis bistortata*
This very common moth flies March/April and again June/August. The colour ranges from very pale grey to dark greyish-brown, but a dark spot is usually visible towards the outer margin of front wing. The larva is brown and feeds on a wide range of trees, including most orchard species. Most Europe.

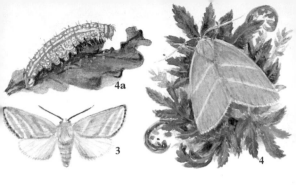

3. Green Silver-lines *Pseudoips fagana*

Easily recognised by its unusual coloration, this moth flies in wooded areas May/July. The reddish margins of wings may be wider than shown here. Female has white hind wings. The larva is green with yellowish dots and lines and red flashes on the claspers. It feeds on oak, beech, birch, and various other trees August/September. N. & C. Europe.

4. Scarce Silver-lines *Bena prasinana*

Although certainly rarer than **3**, this species is not really scarce. It is actually quite common in some of the more extensive forests, where the larva **(4a)** feeds on oak April/May. It pupates in a boat-shaped cocoon attached to a leaf. The adult flies June/July. Hind wings are very white and silky. S. & C. Europe: southern B. only.

1. **Miller Moth** *Apatele leporina*

This moth is named for the very pale wings, which are quite white in many continental specimens. Most British specimens are pale grey, as shown here. It flies May/July. The larva is pale green with a 'wig' of long white hair. It feeds July/September, mainly on birch and alder. Local in much of Europe.

2. **Sycamore Moth** *Apatele aceris*

This rather inconspicuous moth flies June/July. The hind wings are white. The larva **(2a)** feeds on maple and sycamore, and less commonly on plum and certain other trees August/September. It is not uncommon in urban areas where roadside sycamores are grown. Its long, pointed tufts of yellow or reddish hairs give the larva a very spike appearance, especially when it coils up on being disturbed. S. & C. Europe: southern B. only.

3. Grey Dagger *Apatele psi*

This very common moth gets its name from the little dagger-like marks on front wing. It flies May/June and is very well camouflaged when resting on lichen-covered rocks and tree trunks. It is a regular visitor to lights. The larva **(3a)** feeds July/September on hawthorn, birch, plum, and many other trees and shrubs. Most Europe.

4. Dark Dagger *Apatele tridens*

Although this species may be slightly darker, there are no reliable external features to distinguish it from **3**. It is necessary to examine the genitalia for a definite identification. The larvae are quite different, however, as shown in the illustrations. The dark dagger flies June/July, and the larva feeds on oak, birch, hawthorn, and other trees August/October. N. & C. Europe.

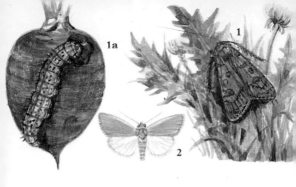

1. **Turnip Moth** *Agrotis segetum*

The front wings of this very common moth range from pale greyish-brown to almost black. Hind wings have a pearly lustre, white in male and greyish in female, which distinguishes the species from most of its relatives. It flies May/June and sometimes again in autumn. The larva **(1a)** feeds mainly underground on turnips and other root crops. It also nibbles through the stems of cabbages and similar crops at ground level. It feeds through the winter and pupates in spring. Most Europe.

2. **Cream-bordered Green Pea** *Earias clorana*

This moth flies in fens and other damp habitats May/August. The larva is pale green with brown lines on the back. It feeds on willow June/September, pulling leaves together with silk to make a retreat. Much of Europe: southern B. only.

3. **Heart and Dart** *Agrotis exclamationis*
Named for the two most prominent markings on its rather drab front wings, this extremely common moth flies May/July and sometimes again in autumn (a 2nd brood is normal in S. Europe). It is abundant in light traps. The larva is brown above and pale below and feeds June onwards on a wide variety of herbaceous plants. Most Europe.

4. **Setaceous Hebrew Character**
Xestia c-nigrum
A very common visitor to light, this species flies May/July and again in autumn. The larva, green at first then becoming brown with black, wedge-shaped marks on the back, feeds on a wide variety of low-growing plants. Some larvae feed up and pupate in autumn to give rise to adults in spring, whereas most larvae feed through the winter and pupate in spring to give autumn adults. Most Europe.

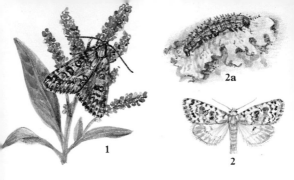

1. **The Knot Grass** *Apatele rumicis*

The front wings vary in the amount of dark colouring and are sometimes almost black, with just the white sub-marginal line and the dots close to the hind margin visible. Hind wings are grey with a darker border. It flies June/September. The hairy larva is dark grey with red and white spots and somewhat angular. It feeds on sallow and bramble and various herbaceous plants July/October. Most Europe.

2. **Marbled Beauty** *Cryphia perla*

This pretty little moth flies June/August and is most often seen at lights. Its mottled greyish or greenish wings make it very difficult to find by day, when it rests on lichen-covered walls and tree-trunks. The larva (**2a**) feeds on lichens August/May. Most Europe.

3

4

3. Flame Shoulder *Ochropleura plecta*

This common moth flies throughout the summer and frequently comes to lights. The larva is greyish brown at first, becoming yellower as it grows, and has a bold pale stripe on each side. It feeds on various low-growing plants all summer. Most Europe.

4. Merveille-du-Jour *Dichonia aprilina*

Although its name means 'wonder of the day', this moth is rarely seen in the daytime because it blends so well with the lichen-covered bark. It flies August/October and is attracted to street lamps and other lights. It occurs wherever oak trees are plentiful. The larva is dark green with a straight white line and two zig-zag black lines down the back. It feeds on oak March/June, boring into an unopened bud at first and moving to the leaves as they open. Most Europe.

1. **Lesser Yellow Underwing** *Noctua comes*

The yellow underwings are all exponents of flash coloration. When disturbed, they fly rapidly away and flash the yellow hindwings. Birds try to follow the yellow, but the moths quickly drop to the ground and 'hide' under the dull front wings. The lesser yellow underwing has front wings ranging from pale greyish-brown to chestnut and dark brown. Hind wing is like that of **3** but has a black spot on front margin. It flies June/September. The robust, greyish larva feeds on a wide range of plants September/April. Most Europe.

2. **Broad-bordered Yellow Underwing**

Noctua fimbriata

Front wings range from pale-greenish brown to deep chestnut. Female is paler than male. It flies June/September. The larva is brown and feeds on various trees autumn and spring. Most Europe.

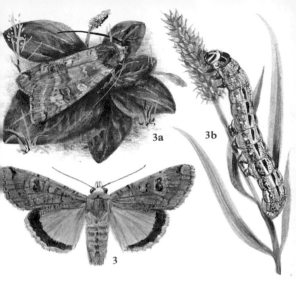

3. Large Yellow Underwing *Noctua pronuba*

An extremely common visitor to light traps, this moth flies May/September. Front wings range from greyish-brown to deep chestnut and almost black. Like **1** and **2**, it rests with its wings folded flat over the back **(3a)** and not roof-like. The larva **(3b)** feeds autumn/spring on a wide variety of herbaceous plants. All Europe. (There are several other similar species of yellow underwings, with broad or narrow margins to hind wings.)

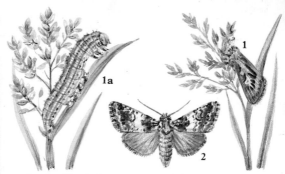

1. **Antler Moth** *Cerapteryx graminis*

An abundant grassland species, this moth flies June/September and is often active by day. It gets its name from the antler-like pattern on front wing, but both pattern and colour vary. Female is much larger than male and usually paler. The larva **(1a)** feeds on grasses in spring and summer and is sometimes so common that it devastates large areas of upland pasture. All Europe.

2. **Varied Coronet** *Hadena compta*

This moth flies June/July, sometimes with a small 2nd brood later. The yellowish-brown larva feeds on the developing seeds of *Dianthus* and related plants. First definitely found in B. in 1948, when large numbers occurred in Dover, it has now spread over S.E. England and East Anglia. The larva feeds mainly on sweet william in B. S. & C. Europe.

3. Common Rustic *Apamea secalis*

This extremely common and variable moth flies June/September and is a frequent visitor to light traps. Front wings range from greyish-brown to chestnut or black, but the pale kidney-shaped mark is nearly always visible. The wings may be elaborately mottled with browns, or else more or less plain. Two of the common forms of the species are shown here. The larva **(3a)** feeds on various grasses as well as on the woodrush shown here autumn/spring. All Europe.

1. **Straw Underwing** *Thalpophila matura*

Named for its pale straw-coloured hind wings, this moth flies June/August and is often an abundant visitor to light traps. Like the yellow underwings (p.180), it flies rapidly when disturbed in the daytime, flashing the pale hind wings as it goes. The larva is dull brown and feeds on grasses September/April. Most Europe.

2. **Broad-barred White** *Hecatera bicolorata*

The ground colour of front wings is usually white, but may be grey, especially in the outer region. Hind wings of male are generally somewhat paler than those of female. It flies May/August. The larva is brownish with a greenish tinge and with a yellowish stripe along the spiracles. It feeds June/August on hawksbeards (*Crepis* spp.). Most Europe: mainly southern B.

3. Cabbage Moth *Mamestra brassicae*

The front wings of this very common moth range from greyish-brown to blackish. The white line near outer margin is absent from most northern specimens. Hind wings are brownish-grey. There is only one brood each year, but emergence takes place over a long period and the adults fly May/September. The larva **(3a)** is a destructive creature, regularly found inside cabbages being prepared for the table. It varies from bright green to olive green and almost black. It does not restrict itself to cabbages and feeds on almost any kind of low-growing plant July/October. It will also eat the leaves of various kinds of trees. All Europe except the far north.

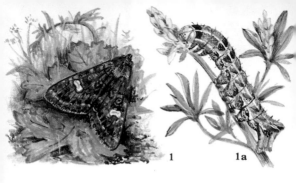

1   1a

1. Dot Moth *Melanchra persicariae*
This is an extremely common insect and is generally
very easily recognised by the prominent white dot on
the blue-black front wing. Some continental specimens lack this dot, however, and the broken pale line
near the wing margin may also be absent in some
individuals. Hind wings are dingy brownish or grey.
It flies June/August and is a regular visitor to light
traps. The larva **(1a)** is commonly pale green with
darker markings but it may be pale brown with dark
brown markings as shown here. It feeds July/
October on a wide variety of herbaceous plants and
shrubs, often in the garden. It is especially fond of
stinging nettles. Much of Europe: mainly southern
B.

2. Bright-line Brown-eye *Lacanobia oleracea*
On the wing May/July, with a small 2nd brood in
southern parts, including southern B., this moth gets
its name from the pattern of the front wing. The
ground colour may be quite dark and the brown 'eye'
is then largely obscured. The larva may be green,
brown, or dark pink, with a prominent grey-edged
yellow stripe along the side. It feeds on stinging
nettle and a wide variety of other herbaceous plants
July/September. Most Europe.

3. *Mamestra cavernosa*
The ground colour of front wing is dark violet-grey
in male, while female is much browner, although she
may be dark grey. Both sexes have a yellowish inner
margin and strong, dark arrow-like markings. Hind
wings are greyish-brown with darker margins. It
flies in June. S. & C. Europe: not B.

1. **Dark Arches** *Apamea monoglypha*

This is a very common and variable species flying
June/August and sometimes again in late autumn. It
is readily attracted to light traps, often arriving in
droves on a humid night. Front wings range from
pale grey with distinct dark markings to almost black.
Few markings are visible on the darker individuals.
The larva (**1a**) feeds on grasses, usually chewing
through the bases of the stems, August/June. Most
Europe.

2. **Light Arches** *Apamea lithoxylaea*

This moth flies June/July and is most often seen
resting on trees and fences. The larva is similar to
that of **1**, but has a brown head. It feeds August/June
on the basal parts of grasses. Most Europe, but not
far north.

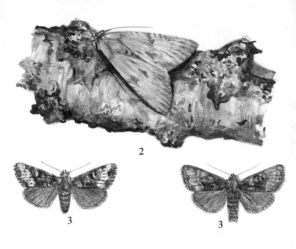

2

3

3

3. Marbled Minor *Oligia strigilis*

This is an extremely common and very variable moth, of which just two forms are illustrated here. It is often difficult to separate this species from some of its close relatives without examining the genitalia. It flies June/July and is much attracted to honeydew and to the entomologist's sugar patch. The larva is purplish-brown above and dull brown below, with pale yellow stripes on the back and along the sides. It hibernates while small and completes its growth on the stems of various grasses in spring. All Europe.

1. Angle Shades
Phlogophora meticulosa

This very common moth flies all year. At rest, wings are creased lengthwise and resemble a dead leaf. The larva is green or brown and fairly stout, with darker V-shaped marks on the back. It feeds throughout the year on almost any kind of herbaceous plant. Most Europe.

2. Rosy Rustic *Hydraecia micacea*

Flying in autumn, this moth is most common in coastal areas. The larva, pinkish-brown with dark brown dots, feeds on various low-growing plants May/August. Most Europe.

3. *Amphipoea fucosa*

Flying June/September, this moth is one of several very similar species. The larva eats grasses and other low-growing plants. N. & C. Europe.

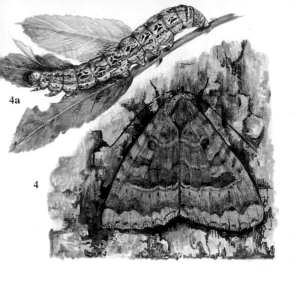

4a

4

4. Old Lady *Mormo maura*

This moth got its name because the wing pattern was thought to resemble the dark shawls worn by elderly Victorian ladies. Hind wings are equally sombre. It flies June/September and frequently enters houses and barns to rest in the daytime. The larva **(4a)** ranges from grey to purplish-brown and feeds on low-growing plants before hibernation. In spring it turns its attention to sallow and other trees and shrubs. Most Europe: mainly southern B.

1. Beaded Chestnut *Agrochola lychnidis*

Front wings of this common moth range from pale
brown to deep orange-brown or brick-red. Typically,
they are mottled, as shown here, but they may be
plain-coloured with just a few black dots. The dots
on front edge are usually quite obvious. It flies
September/November. The larva, green above and
yellowish below, feeds on various plants April/May.
Most Europe.

2. Malachite Moth *Calotaenia celsia*

This beautiful insect flies in the autumn in open
coniferous woods, generally on sandy soils. The larva
is rather like that of the dark arches (p.188), yellowish
green with black tubercles but with a brown head. It
feeds at the bases of various grasses during summer.
N. & C. Europe, especially in eastern regions: not B.

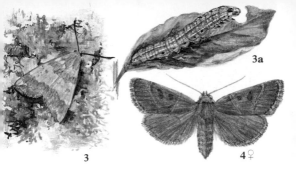

3

3a

4 ♀

3. Barred Sallow *Xanthia aurago*

The ground colour of this attractive moth is usually pale yellow, as shown here, but it may be deep yellow or even bright orange. The darker bands range from purplish-brown to red. Occasionally the wings are uniformly orange. The moth flies September/October, usually in the vicinity of beech woods. The larva (3a) feeds on beech and maple April/June, beginning with buds and moving to the leaves as they open. S. & C. Europe: mainly southern B.

4. *Pseudenargia ulicis*

The front wing ranges from reddish-brown to greenish-brown. Hind wing of male is whitish, while that of female is dingy brown, but both sexes bear a rosy tinge. It flies in the autumn. The larva feeds on gorse in the spring, surrounding itself with a silken web. Spain.

1. The Clay *Mythimna ferrago*

Also known as the clay wainscot, this common moth frequently comes to lighted windows June/August. Seen from below – through the window, for example – male can be recognised by a tuft of black hair at base of abdomen. Front wings range from pinkish-grey to rust-brown. Hind wings are smoky brown. The brownish larva feeds on grasses and other low-growing plants autumn and spring. Most Europe.

2. Smoky Wainscot *Mythimna impura*

The smoky hind wings together with the dark stripe through centre of front wing distinguish this common moth from several similar species. It flies June/September. The larva is pale brown, with a greenish tinge below and white lines along the back. It feeds on grasses, hibernating when small and completing growth in spring. Most Europe.

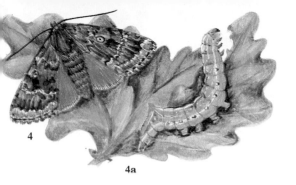

4

4a

3. **Frosted Orange** *Gortyna flavago*

This attractive, but rarely seen moth flies July/October in marshy habitats. Female is a little paler. The larva is pale brown and feeds in stems of thistles, hemp agrimony, and other marsh-loving plants April/August. Most Europe.

4. **Copper Underwing** *Amphipyra pyramidea*

Named for the beautiful copper colour of hind wings, this moth flies July/October. The larva **(4a)** feeds March/June on various trees and shrubs, especially oak, birch, and sallow. S. & C. Europe: mainly southern B. (In 1967 it was discovered that copper underwings actually belong to two distinct species – *A. pyramidea* and *A. berbera*. They are very alike, but *pyramidea* has a fairly distinct chequer-board pattern on the sides of the abdomen, while *berbera* has just a plain black suffusion.)

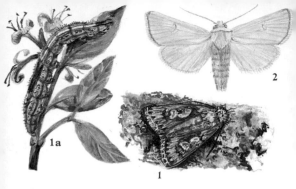

1. **Early Grey** *Xylocampa areola*

This well-named moth flies March/May, when it feeds by night at the catkins of sallow bushes. When resting by day, it is difficult to detect on walls and lichen-covered tree trunks. Occasional darker specimens occur, and some have a rosy tinge. Hind wings are light grey. The larva (**1a**) feeds on honeysuckle May/July. Most Europe except far north.

2. *Calamia virens*

This beautiful moth sometimes has the white kidney-shaped mark edged with rusty brown. Hind wing of female is whitish-green, and paler than that of male. It flies late summer and early autumn. The eggs hatch in spring and the larva feeds on plantains and other low-growing plants. It is dark greenish-brown with a pale line along the back and black spots. S. & C. Europe: not B.

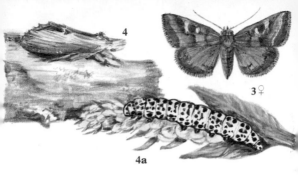

4

3 ♀

4a

3. *Synthymia fixa*

This moth flies in dry, hilly areas in spring. The front wing of male is ash-grey, while that of female is darker and slightly greenish. Hind wing is paler in male. The larva is dark green, with yellow and white lines, and feeds on pitch trefoil in summer. S. Europe.

4. **Mullein Moth** *Cucullia verbasci*

When at rest with wings pulled back along the body, this moth bears a remarkable resemblance to a sliver of wood or bark. It flies April/June. Female is slightly less boldly marked than male. The very conspicuous larva **(4a)** advertises its unpleasant taste with bold warning coloration. It feeds June/July, fully exposed on the leaves and shoots of mullein plants. It often destroys entire flower spikes. S. & C. Europe: mainly southern B.

1. The Sword-grass *Xylena exsoleta*
This moth flies for most of the autumn and then
hibernates. It flies again March/May. The handsome
larva is bright green with black spots and red, white,
and yellow stripes. It feeds April/June on dock,
groundsel, and other low-growing plants. Most
Europe: commonest in northern B. (The red sword-
grass (*X. vetusta*) is similar but front wings are
darker and more reddish-brown.)

2. The Shark *Cucullia umbratica*
Flying May/July, this moth likes to visit honeysuckle and other flowers. By day, it rests on trees and
fences, pulling the wings tightly back against the
body and looking like a sliver of wood. The larva is
greyish-brown with a pattern of black dots. It feeds
on sowthistle and other composites June/September.
Most Europe.

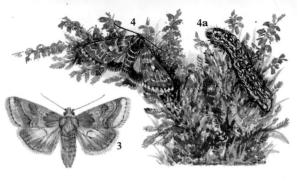

3. Pease-blossom *Periphanes delphinii*
This very pretty little moth flies April/June. Female is darker, with a greyish cast on all wings. The larva is violet-grey with yellow and black lines. It feeds on larkspur and delphiniums July/August. S. & C. Europe, occasionally wandering northwards: just a few old records from B.

4. Beautiful Yellow Underwing *Anarta myrtilli*
Front wings of this attractive moth may vary, but are always a fairly bright shade of brown, generally with plenty of red in it. This distinguishes it from the small dark yellow underwing (*A. cordigera*), which has blackish brown front wings and also a darker hind wing margin. It inhabits heaths and moorland, flying by day April/September. There are two broods in the south. The larva (**4a**) feeds June/September on heather. All Europe.

1. **Golden Plusia** *Polychrisia moneta*

This attractive moth flies June/September, with one or two broods, and is regularly seen at garden flowers and at lights. The larva is bright green with a dark line on the back and a white one on each side. It feeds on a variety of plants on the continent, but mainly delphinium, larkspur, and monkshood in B. It spins leaves and flower heads together to form a shelter. It was not found in B. until 1890, but now occurs in most parts. Most Europe.

2. **Gold Spangle** *Autographa bractea*

Easily recognised by the large metallic spangle on each front wing, this moth flies June/August. The larva is green with indistinct white lines and feeds on a wide variety of plants August/May. It hibernates when very small. N. & C. Europe: mainly northern and western B.

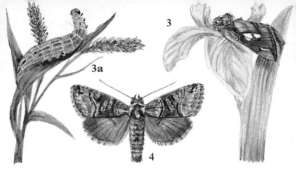

3. Gold Spot *Plusia festucae*

The ground colour of front wings ranges from golden brown to chestnut. It flies May/July, sometimes with a 2nd brood August/September. The larva (**3a**) feeds on sedges, various grasses, and other waterside plants April/August. Like the larvae of **1** & **2**, it has only two pairs of prolegs in addition to the claspers. Much of Europe: mainly northern B.

4. The Spectacle *Abrostola triplasia*

When seen head-on, the pattern of thoracic hairs resembles a pair of spectacles. It flies May/August and regularly visits lights. The larva is pale green and rather angular, with white stripes and some darker chevron marks on the back. It feeds on stinging nettle June/September. Most Europe. (The dark spectacle (*A. trigemina*) is darker, with brownish instead of grey 'spectacles'.)

1. Herald Moth *Scoliopteryx libatrix*
This most attractive moth flies August/October, when it can be seen feeding at ivy blossom and other flowers, and then goes into hibernation in hollow trees, barns, and attics. It sleeps for about six months and is on the wing again March/June. It thus has a very long adult life. In both spring and autumn it is commonly attracted to lighted windows. The larva **(1a)** feeds on willows and poplars June/August. All Europe.

2. Spotted Sulphur *Emmelia trabealis*
This very easily recognised moth flies June/August and is usually on the wing late afternoon and early evening. There are two broods. The black markings vary in number and depth of colour. The larva is reddish brown and feeds on bindweed July/September. S. & C. Europe: mainly eastern B.

3. Scarce Burnished Brass *Diachrysia chryson*
The single more or less square brassy patch on the
front wing distinguishes this moth from **4**. It flies
June/August, usually in fens and other damp places.
The larva feeds on hemp agrimony in August and
then hibernates before completing growth May/June.
When mature it is yellowish green with darker and
lighter stripes. It has only two pairs of prolegs plus
the claspers. Much of Europe: rare in B. (south
only).

4. Burnished Brass *Diachrysia chrysitis*
This very common species flies May/September,
often with two broods. It is regularly attracted to
lights. The pattern varies a little and the metallic
areas may be golden or quite green. Like the related
silver-Y and golden-Y moths, it has several crests or
tufts of hair on the thorax. These are very prominent
in both frontal and lateral views. The larva resembles
that of **3**, but is more bluish green. It feeds on
stinging nettle and deadnettle in summer and again
after hibernation. Most Europe.

1. Silver-Y Moth *Autographa gamma*

Named for the silvery Y-shaped mark on front wing, this very active moth flies at all times of day and night. The ground colour ranges from pale grey to velvety black. Like the other moths on this page and the closely related burnished brass (p.203), its thorax is decorated with prominent tufts and crowns of hair. It is a strong migrant, often travelling in large swarms, and it moves northwards each spring to invade B. and northern Europe, where it multiplies rapidly and builds up large populations by late summer. It can then be seen feeding on all kinds of flowers, its wings rarely ceasing to vibrate even when it alights to feed. The larva **(1a)** may be pale or dark green and it feeds on almost any low-growing plant throughout the summer. All Europe, but it cannot survive the winter in B. and other northern regions.

2. Beautiful Golden-Y *Autographa pulchrina*

Flying May/August, this species can be separated from **3** by the clear gold-edged kidney-shaped mark just above the golden Y. The latter is not always a complete Y and it sits on a rather broken and indistinct dark patch. The cross-line just beyond the patch bends inwards near the front margin. The larva, green with white stripes, feeds on various low-growing plants July/September and again after hibernation. Most Europe.

3. Plain Golden-Y *Autographa jota*

Front wings have a large, even patch of dark colour enclosing the Y. The latter is usually, but not always, broken into a V and a dot. The kidney-shaped mark is indistinct and the cross-line does not curve inwards as in **2**. It flies May/August. The larva is like that of **2** and feeds on a wide variety of plants. Most Europe.

1

2

1. *Syngrapha ain*

The front wings of this moth resemble those of the silver-Y (p.204), but hind wings are more like those of a yellow underwing (p.180) – bright yellow with a dark border. It flies July/August. The larva is a beautiful green with pale lines and it blends perfectly with the larch needles on which it feeds. It begins feeding in the autumn, but then goes into hibernation until about May before completing its growth. Alps and other mountains of C. Europe: not B.

2. Slender Burnished Brass
Diachrysia orichalcea
This very attractive moth, a close relative of the burnished brass (p.203), flies in the summer. The larva is bluish-green with white lines and it feeds on various composites in autumn and again after hibernation in spring. Like that of **1**, it has only three pairs of prolegs, including the claspers. S. Europe, but occasional vagrants reach B. and other parts of N. & C. Europe.

3. Mother Shipton *Callistege mi*

The front wing of this sombre, day-flying moth bears a prominent M-shaped mark which, viewed from the right angle, resembles a grotesque face. Once called the mask moth, it got its present name from the resemblance of the mark to the witch-like profile of the legendary prophetess Mother Shipton. Hind wings are black with white or cream spots. It flies May/July in flowery places. The larva (**3a**) feeds on grasses and clovers July/September. Most Europe except far north.

4. Burnet Companion *Euclidia glyphica*

This common day-flying moth inhabits rough, flowery grassland May/July. It often flies with **3**, as well as with the burnet moths which give it its name. The larva resembles that of **3** and eats clovers and trefoils July/August. Most Europe.

1   2

1. Beautiful Hook-tip *Laspeyria flexula*

Unrelated to the true hook-tips (p.138), this moth
flies along hedgerows and woodland margins June/
August. The colour varies from greyish-brown to
purplish-brown, but is always sprinkled with black
dots. The larva is bluish-green with darker green
points on the back. There are also some black-tipped
'warts', and the spiracles are ringed with brown. The
lower edges of the body carry fringes of pale, fleshy
filaments which help to conceal shadows when the
larva is resting on twigs. It feeds September/May on
lichens growing on various trees. C. Europe: southern B. only.

2. The Alchymist *Catephia alchymista*

This species is on the wing May/June and occurs
mainly in wooded regions. The larva is reddish-
brown with pairs of prominent black tubercles on
the back and a pair of pointed outgrowths on the 5th
and 12th segments. It feeds on oak July/August. S. &
C. Europe: a casual visitor to B.

3

4

3. *Ephesia fulminea*

The front wings range from pale to dark grey, with a lilac tinge. The pattern varies a little, and the moth is easily confused with **4**. The black ring in basal half of hind wing may be interrupted in the lower part. The moth flies June/August and seems to be declining. The larva is ash-grey or brown with prominent tubercles and a horn on 9th segment. It feeds May/June on various trees and shrubs, especially blackthorn and oak. S. & C. Europe: not B.

4. *Ephesia nymphaea*

The crinkled black line around margin of front wing is usually much stronger than in **3**. Hind wing does not normally have a dark ring, as the inner margin generally lacks a dark streak. It flies in July. The larva is yellow, with rust-coloured spots and no horn. It feeds on oak. S. Europe.

1

1. *Anua tirhaca*

This striking moth flies in fairly dry habitats May/
June. Hind wing is deep yellow with a dark border
which is broader in female than in male. The border
is occasionally reduced to a small blotch, and sometimes absent altogether. The larva is reddish-brown
or greyish-brown, with fine dark lines along the
back. It feeds July/August on the mastic tree (*Pistachia
lentiscus*), the sumac, and various species of *Cistus*. S.
Europe.

2

2. Red Underwing *Catocala nupta*

Like the yellow underwing (p.180), this moth displays a very effective flash coloration, exposing its red hind wings as it flies on a rather irregular course, and then dropping down to conceal itself under the sombre front wings. Female is often a little larger and darker. It is one of several similar species. It flies July/October. The larva is greyish-brown and twig-like, with numerous 'warts'. It feeds on poplar and willow April/July. It is remarkably well concealed when at rest on a twig: a hair-like fringe hangs down on each side and obliterates the shadows between larva and twig. Most Europe.

1. The Snout *Hypena proboscidalis*

Named for the prominent palps which project forward from the head at rest, this moth flies June/July, sometimes with a partial 2nd brood in autumn. It can be found in all kinds of rough places where stinging nettles grow and it usually takes to the wing early in the evening. The larva **(1a)** feeds on stinging nettles May/June. Most Europe.

2. The Fan-foot *Polypogon tarsipennalis*

Flying June/July, this little moth inhabits hedgerows and light woodland. It gets its name because male has a slender tuft of hair on front leg. Male antenna also has a swelling near the middle. The larva is greyish-brown with darker freckles and three darker lines on the back. It feeds on a wide range of plants July/August, hibernating when nearly full-grown and completing its growth in spring. Most Europe.

3

3. **Clifden Nonpareil** *Catocala fraxini*

This handsome relative of the red underwing (p.211) flies July/September and, like its relatives, it is readily attracted to light. At rest, it is very well camouflaged on tree trunks. The larva is brownish-grey and resembles a fairly stout twig, but it does not have such well-developed shadow-hiding fringes as the red underwing larva. It feeds on poplar, willow, and ash May/July. C. Europe: a rare visitor to B.

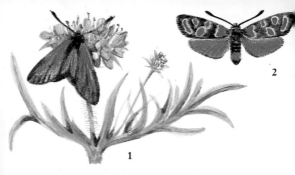

The burnets are day-flying moths, generally coloured black and red as a warning to birds that they are poisonous. Their bodies actually contain cyanide. They have clubbed antennae and are often confused with butterflies, but their wings are joined with a frenulum (see p.8) and they are clearly moths. They are rather lethargic, heavy bodied insects and can often be picked up while feeding at flowers. Flight is rather slow and silent, although the wings beat quite rapidly. The larvae generally pupate in papery cocoons.

1. *Zygaena osterodensis*
This moth has rather longer and more slender antennae than most other burnets. It flies June/July in upland meadows and, unlike most burnets, it readily flies when disturbed. The larva is of the typical burnet shape (see p.217) and is golden yellow with black and white spots. Most Europe: not B.

2. *Zygaena carniolica*

This very common and variable moth flies June/August in open woodland and scrub. The abdominal red belt may be absent. The larva is bluish-green with white lines and yellow and black dots. It feeds on various legumes in spring. S. & C. Europe: not B. (It is often confused with *Z. fausta*, but the latter is basically red with small black markings and a broader red belt.)

3. *Zygaena ephialtes*

The basal two spots on front wings are usually red and the rest are usually white, but the outer spot may be red. Hind wing normally has a white spot. The species is very variable, however, and all the red may be replaced by yellow in Austria and northern Italy. This form (**3a**) is sub-species *coronillae*. Hind wings may also be yellow. It flies June/July. The larva is yellowish-green with orange sides, a black dorsal stripe, and black spots. It feeds in spring on vetches, trefoils, thyme, plantains, and other low-growing plants. S. & C. Europe: not B.

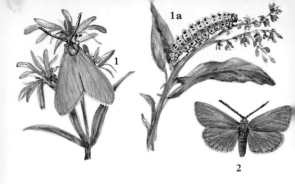

1. **Common Forester** *Adscita statices*

This metallic, day-flying moth is related to the burnets, but its antennae are toothed and not clubbed. Front wings are typically bluish-green, but are mainly bronzy-green in B. It flies May/July in grassy places, especially in damp areas where it enjoys the flowers of ragged robin. The larva (**1a**) feeds on sorrel in autumn and again after hibernation. Most Europe: mainly southern B.

2. *Aglaope infausta*

This rather transparent, smoky-winged moth flies in the July sunshine in rough, scrubby places. Unlike the related foresters and burnets, it has no tongue and is not attracted to flowers. The short, stout larva feeds on blackthorn and hawthorn and probably other rosaceous plants. S. & C. Europe: not B.

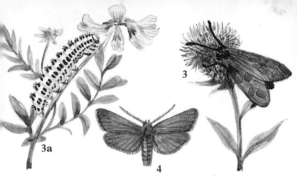

3. Six-spot Burnet *Zygaena filipendulae*

This is one of the commonest and most typical burnets, flying in grassy and flowery places May/August. Large numbers often cluster on knapweed and scabious flowers. Front wings are deep metallic green with red spots. The two outer spots often fuse together. Hind wing is bright red with a black border. All red is occasionally replaced by yellow. The larva **(3a)** feeds on trefoils and other leguminous plants in autumn and again after hibernation. All Europe. (The five-spot burnet (*Z. trifolii*) is very similar but has only five spots on front wing.)

4. *Rhagades pruni*

The front wings of this moth range from green to blue. It flies in summer. The larva is grey and yellow with red spots and feeds on heather and *Prunus* spp in spring. C. Europe: not B.

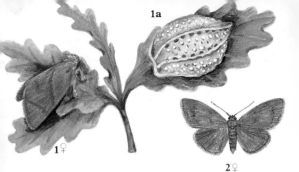

1. The Festoon *Apoda avellana* (× 1¼)

This moth flies in and around oak woods June/July, often circling the tree-tops in the sunshine. Male is smaller and front wings are much darker. Hind wings are darker than front in both sexes. The strange, slug-like larva **(1a)** feeds on oak August/October. It has no prolegs and clings to the leaves by means of its sucker-like underside. S. & C. Europe: southern B. only.

2. The Triangle *Heterogenea asella* (× 1¼)

A close relative of **1**, this little moth flies in sunshine June/July, mainly in beechwoods. Male is smaller and darker than female. The larva resembles that of **1** in shape and is pale green with a reddish-brown mark rather like a spear-head on the back. It feeds on beech, oak, and birch in autumn. C. Europe: southern England only.

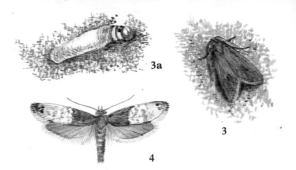

3. Case-bearing Clothes Moth

Tinea pellionella (×2·5)

This familiar household pest is so named because the larva **(3a)** surrounds itself with a portable silken case, to which it attaches fragments of other materials. It is, of course, the larva that damages fabrics, but it eats only animal materials, such as wool, hair, and feathers. It lives in the nests of birds and other animals as well as in houses. The adult flies mainly in summer. Hind wings have long fringes. All Europe.

4. Tapestry Moth *Trichophaga tapetzella* (×2)

This is one of the largest of the fabric-damaging species. The larva eats only animal fibres and damages furs and coarse woollen fabrics. It thrives best in damp places and often feeds on horse-hair in stables. The adult flies mainly June/July, but the larva occurs throughout the year. All Europe.

1. Goat Moth *Cossus cossus*

This large species gets its name because the larva emits a pungent, goat-like smell. Female is larger than male, with broader wings and a bulkier body. It flies June/August in wooded habitats, where it may be found resting on tree trunks and fence posts by day, although it is easily overlooked because of its sombre colouring. The larva ranges from deep pink to chestnut and feeds in the trunks of various trees, especially willows, for three or four years before maturing. Most Europe.

2. *Dyspessa ulula*

This little moth varies a good deal in the pattern and depth of colour of the wings, but is usually easy to recognise. It inhabits sandy places and flies May/July. The larva lives in onion bulbs and hibernates twice before maturing. Local in S. & C. Europe from S. Germany southwards.

3. **Reed Leopard** *Phragmataecia castaneae*
This moth flies in fens and other damp habitats June/July. Female is somewhat larger than male and has simple antennae. The larva is yellowish white with reddish brown stripes and feeds in reed stems for nearly two years. Local in C. Europe: rare in B.

4. **Leopard Moth** *Zeuzera pyrina*
The wings of this species are thinly scaled and always look worn. It flies June/August and is often attracted to street lights. Female is larger than male and often more heavily spotted. Male antennae are feathery in basal half, but those of female are thread-like throughout. The larva, yellowish-white with black spots, feeds for two or three years in the trunks and branches of various trees. Most Europe.

1. Hornet Clearwing *Sesia apiformis*

The members of the clearwing family are day-flying moths in which the wings are largely devoid of scales and therefore largely transparent. The antennae of most species thicken towards the tip. The moths display some striking resemblances to various bees and wasps, thereby gaining protection from birds. The larvae are rather maggot-like and most live and feed inside stems and roots. The hornet clearwing resembles a hornet in flight, although it rests with wings half spread and not folded along the back. It flies May/July. The larva feeds in the roots and trunks of poplars, taking two years to mature. Most Europe.

2. Dusky Clearwing *Paranthrene tabaniformis*

Supposedly resembling a horse-fly, this moth flies June/August. The larva feeds for two years in the roots and trunks of poplars. Much of Europe, but local: v. rare in B (southern counties only).

3. Red-belted Clearwing *Conopia myopaeformis*
The abdominal belt of this moth is normally red, but
may be orange or yellow. It flies June/August and is
not uncommon in orchards and gardens. The larva
feeds in trunks and branches of apple and pear and,
like most clearwing larvae, takes two years to mature.
Much of Europe: southern B. only.

4. Welsh Clearwing *Conopia scoliaeformis*
Named because the first British specimen was found
in Wales, this moth actually has a wide distribution.
The orange anal tuft distinguishes it from most other
clearwings. It flies June/August. The larva feeds for
two years in birch trunks. N. & C. Europe, but very
local: rare in B.

5. Lunar Hornet Clearwing
Sphecia bembeciformis
Distinguished from **1** by the narrow yellow collar
and the lack of yellow patches on the 'shoulders', this
handsome moth flies in wooded areas June/July.
Like the other clearwing moths, it is most often
found sunning itself on the vegetation. The larva
feeds in the stems of various willows and poplars. C.
Europe.

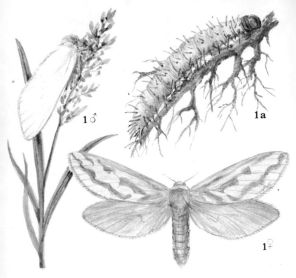

1. Ghost Swift *Hepialus humuli*

The swift moths are rather primitive moths whose front and hind wings are of similar shape and size. Flight is usually rapid. The antennae are very small. Female is generally larger than male. The male ghost swift is white above and dark brown below. It flies at dusk June/August, slowly rising and falling. The ghost-like white flashes of the wings attract female. The larva (**1a**) feeds on the roots of various plants July/May. N. & C. Europe.

2

3

2. Map-winged Swift *Hepialus fusconebulosa*
The pale wing markings which give this species its name are very variable and may be almost absent, especially in the north and west. The moth flies June/August, usually at dusk. It inhabits heathland and bracken-covered hillsides. The larva, similar to that of **1**, feeds on bracken rhizomes for almost two years before pupating. Most Europe.

3. Common Swift *Hepialus lupulinus*
The wings of this very common species vary from almost white to deep brown, and the white markings are also very variable. It flies at dusk April/July and often visits lights, whirring around them with a fast and furious flight. At rest, it resembles a broken twig. As with all swift moths, the female simply scatters her eggs over the vegetation. The shiny white larva feeds July/April on the roots of a wide variety of plants and is sometimes a pest. N. & C. Europe and also S.E. Europe.

1. *Sterrhopterix fusca* (×2)

This rarely-seen insect is one of the bagworm moths, so-called because the larvae build cases of plant fragments held together with silk. The case **(1a)** is carried about by the larva and fixed to a leaf or twig before pupation. The male flies by day June/July, but female is wingless and does not even leave her larval case to mate or lay eggs. The larva feeds on various trees August/May. C. Europe.

2. Gold Swift *Hepialus hecta*

This moth flies May/July in places where bracken grows. Male has a hovering flight. Female is much paler and less strongly marked. The larvae feed on bracken rhizomes for nearly two years and then complete their growth in young shoots before pupating in May. As with all swift moths, the pupal stage is very short. N. & C. Europe.

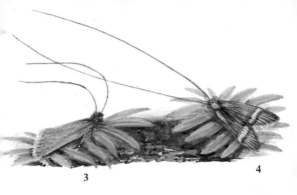

3 4

3. *Adela reaumurella* (×2)

This day-flying moth is on the wing May/June. Males swarm around oaks and other trees in the sunshine and wave their long antennae as they sit on the foliage. Female antennae are not much longer than front wing and largely black. Hind wings are purplish-brown with bronze fringes. The larva builds a small flat case of leaf fragments and feeds among leaf litter September/March. Most Europe.

4. *Nemophora degeerella* (×2)

Although closely related to **3**, this moth flies at dusk. It swarms in damp woodland May/June. Male antennae are longer than in any other British lepidoptera. Female antennae are only just longer than front wing. The larva feeds on leaf litter in a case of leaf fragments. Most Europe.

1. Small Magpie *Eurrhypara hortulata* ($\times 1\frac{3}{4}$)
This delicate moth, which is no relation of the magpie moth (p.158), takes to the wing at dusk June/July and often comes to lighted windows. It is also easily disturbed amongst rank herbage and undergrowth by day. The flesh-coloured larva (**1a**) feeds mainly on stinging nettle, rolling the leaves up to form a shelter. It can be found August/September. Most Europe.

2. European Corn Borer *Ostrinia nubilalis* ($\times 1\frac{1}{4}$)
Flying May/August, this moth gets its name because on the continent and in North America the larva bores into maize stems and causes serious damage. It will, however, tunnel into the stems of a very wide range of plants. Female is much paler and sometimes bright yellow on the continent. Much of Europe: sporadic visitor to B.

3. *Scoparia dubitalis* (×2)

One of several very similar species, this little moth flies May/July, mainly in coastal areas and over rough grassland. At rest, the wings are swept back to form a narrow triangle, with the head and palps forming a sharp point at the front. The larva feeds on the roots of various plants. Most Europe.

4. White Plume Moth

Pterophorus pentadactylus (×1¾)

This common visitor to lighted windows June/July is also easily disturbed from the herbage during the day. The wings are divided into five feathery plumes on each side. The hairy green larva feeds on hedge bindweed, hibernating while small and completing growth in spring. Most Europe: rarer in north. (There are several other plume moths, mostly with brown wings. Their wings are not always deeply divided, and some are not divided at all.)

1. Mother-of-Pearl Moth

Pleuroptya ruralis ($\times 1\frac{1}{4}$)

This aptly-named moth is most often seen drifting ghost-like over nettles and other rough vegetation at dusk June/August. It readily comes to light and is easily beaten from herbage in the daytime. The larva is light green and it feeds on stinging nettles, spinning leaves together to form a shelter. It pupates in such a shelter when fully grown May/June. Most Europe.

2. *Eurrhypara coronata* ($\times 1\frac{1}{4}$)

On the wing May/July, this dainty moth flies in the vicinity of elder trees. Like its relatives on this page, it readily takes flight when disturbed by day, but flight is weak and the moth soon finds another hiding place. The larva is pale green with darker green lines and feeds on elder July/September. It hides by day in a silken web spun on the underside of a leaf. Most Europe.

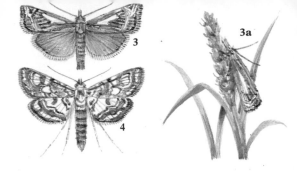

3. *Crambus pratellus* ($\times 1\frac{1}{4}$)

One of the many closely related species known as grass moths, this insect flies May/August in all kinds of grassy places. At rest, it wraps its wings round the body and clings to a grass stem, sometimes head up (**3a**), but more often head down. In such a position it is hard to see. The larva feeds on grass stems in summer. Most Europe.

4. *Nymphula nymphaeaeta* ($\times 1\frac{1}{4}$)

This rather variable species is one of the china-marks moths, so called because their wing patterns resemble the marks which potters put under plates and other china articles. It flies at dusk May/August and hides in waterside herbage by day. The larva feeds on various water plants, living inside floating leaves at first and then making a case of leaf fragments in which it lives on the underside of the leaves. Most Europe.

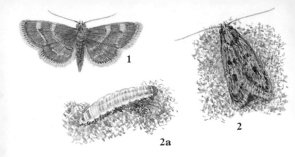

1

2a

2

1. Gold Fringe *Hypsopygia costalis* (×1¼)
This pretty little moth flies July/October. It rests
with wings wide open and pressed against the surface, with hind edge of front wing at right angles to
the body. It is common in and around hedgerows.
The larva is whitish with a dark brown head and it
feeds September/May on dead grasses and other
plants, including stored hay and straw and even roof
thatch. Much of Europe.

2. Brown House Moth
Hofmannophila pseudospretella (×2)
This common household insect resembles the clothes
moths but is a little larger. Hind wings are whitish-
grey. It flies throughout the summer. The larva **(2a)**
feeds on a wide range of both animal and plant
materials, including woollen and cotton fibres as
well as stored seeds and flour. It commonly feeds on
the debris in birds' nests, but can survive only in
fairly damp places. All Europe.

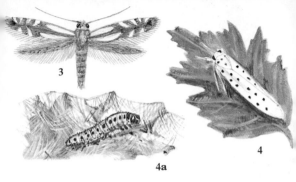

3

4a

4

3. *Phyllonorycter alnifoliella* (×4)

Flying May and August, with two generations, this is one of several closely related and very similar moths. It rests with the wings rolled around the body and turned up slightly at the hind end. The larva tunnels in the leaves of alder in July and again September/October. N. & C. Europe.

4. *Yponomeuta padella* (×2)

One of several very similar moths known as ermels or small ermines, this species flies July/August. Hind wings are dark grey. The larva is greenish-grey with black spots and a black head. It feeds communally on hawthorn and blackthorn in spring. The larvae (**4a**) surround themselves with large silken webs, or tents, and are sometimes so common that whole bushes and even hedgerows are covered with the webs. Most Europe.

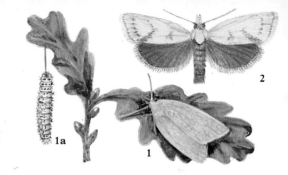

1. Green Oak Tortrix *Tortrix viridana* (×2)
This very common moth flies June/July and when at
rest may be confused with the cream-bordered green
pea (p.176). Hind wings of the latter are white, however, while those of the tortrix are grey. The tortrix
also has markedly rectangular wings, in common
with **2** and **3** and its many other relatives. The larva
(**1a**) feeds mainly on oak April/June. It starts with
the buds and then moves to the leaves, which it folds
or rolls up to form shelters. If a branch is shaken,
large numbers of larvae may drop down on silken
threads. Whole trees may be defoliated in some
years. Most Europe, wherever oaks grow.

2. *Agapeta hamana* (×2)
This pretty moth flies June/August. It rests with its
wings held steeply roofwise over the body. The larva
feeds on the roots of thistles. Most Europe.

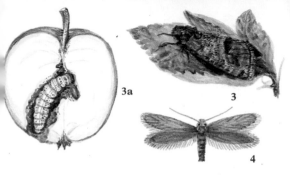

3. Codlin Moth *Cydia pomonella* (×2)

Flying May/July and sometimes again in autumn, this very common moth is found wherever apples grow. Hind wings are dingy brown. The larva **(3a)** bores into young apples and feeds on the developing seeds and surrounding flesh. When fully grown in late summer it chews its way out again and spins a cocoon in a bark crevice. It will also eat pears and a few other fruits. All Europe.

4. *Micropterix calthella* (×4)

This tiny moth is one of a group which have functional jaws instead of tubular mouthparts. It feeds on pollen and is most often seen sitting on the flower heads of sedges and on marsh marigold flowers May/June. The wings are pulled back along the body when at rest and they shine in the sun. It likes moist habitats. The larva lives in the soil, feeding largely on decaying plant matter. All Europe.

Index

Butterflies

236

Moths